BORROWED WARE

Medieval Persian Epigrams

INTRODUCTION
AND TRANSLATION BY
Dick Davis

MAGE PUBLISHERS
WASHINGTON, DC
1997

Persian calligraphy by Amir Hossein Tabnak

English language edition first published in 1996 by
Anvil Press Poetry Ltd
69 King George Street London SE10 8PX

Library of Congress Cataloging-in Publication Data

Davis, Dick, 1945— Borrowed Ware: medieval Persian Epigrams /
introduction and translation by Dick Davis
Text in English, with epigrams in Persian
and English Translation. Includes Index
1. Epigrams, Persian—Translation into English.
2. Epigrams, Persian.
3. Persian Poetry—Translation into English.
4. Persian poetry. I. Title.
PK6449.E5D38 1997
891'. 551208—DC21
97-26837 CIP

ISBN 0-934211-52-3 (cloth : alk. paper)

Mage's books are available through better bookstores or directly from
the publisher. Call toll-free 800-962-0922 for a catalog. Visit Mage
online at www.mage.com. E-mail: Mage1@access.digex.net
Telephone: 202-342-1642 Fax: 202-342-9269

Loe here I showe, this slender woorke and bare,
    In which the paine, but not the prayse is myne;
    Lyke Grapes that grew uppon anothers vyne,
And happly in the gathering brused are.
I cannot bost, but as of borrowed ware,
    Though Grape be good, the Presse may marre the wyne;
    And make it sow're, before it should be fyne,
To please your tast, I did it first prepare:
With higher witts, and woorkes, I not compare ...

— THE ARUNDEL HARINGTON MANUSCRIPT
OF TUDOR POETRY, POEM 228

ACKNOWLEDGEMENTS

Some of these translations have appeared in two chapbooks published by R. L. Barth, *Let Them Be Changed* (1989), and *Borrowed Ware* (1990). Others have appeared in *Drastic Measures; The Epigrammatist; PN Review; Numbers; The Spectator; Spectrum; A Few Friends: Poems for Thom Gunn's Sixtieth Birthday* (Stonyground Press); *Celebrations at Sixty: For Turner Cassity* (R. L. Barth); *The Music of his History: Poems for Charles Gullans on his Sixtieth Birthday* (R. L. Barth); *A Kind of Love: Selected and New Poems* (University of Arkansas Press).

BORROWED WARE

Medieval Persian Epigrams

CONTENTS

Introduction

Above all, poetry lulls them, that genius seeming properly to delight itself
amongst them ... Nor have I read that amongst the Romans, or in any other
parts, poetry has been better rewarded; witness poet Mervan, who for those 70
distichs which he presented Mahomet, the great Almansor's son, received as a
reward 70,000 staters ... And their graceful shaking their notes in chanting
and quavering (after the French air) gives it to the ear harmonious ...

— THOMAS HERBERT, Travels in Persia 1627-9

THE POEMS TRANSLATED HERE were written in Persian between the
10th and late 16th centuries, i.e. throughout what is regarded as
the "classic" period of Persian poetry—in fact extending some-
what beyond its limit, as the period is conventionally held to have
come to an end with the death of the narrative poet Jami in 1492.

There is another limitation of which the reader should be
aware. Persian poetry divides very roughly into three kinds,
according to the poems' length: long (narrative), medium (lyric
and panegyric), and short (epigrammatic: encapsulating a mood,
insight, complaint, compliment or witticism). A selection of the
last kind only—the short epigrammatic poem—is translated here.
This means that many of the most admired poets of Persia
(Nezami, Ferdowsi, Jami for example) are not represented at all in
this volume, and that others (Khaghani, Hafez, Sana'i for exam-
ple) are represented by poems that are not particularly typical of
their total output. That said, the anthology does, I believe, give a
fair idea of the atmosphere and variety of Persian epigrams, and it
also incidentally provides what I hope are fascinating occasional
glimpses into a vanished and extraordinary way of life, that of the
Persian medieval courts. How very like us they were, and also
how utterly unlike, are both apparent in these poems.

Virtually all the poems included can be considered "court"
poems of one kind or another. The first poems to be written in

"modern" Persian (that is in the language that developed after the 7th-century Arab invasion and took literary form in the late 9th century) were panegyrics—praise poems—of local rulers. There is a story, which may even be true, of how one such ruler in eastern Iran, whose command of Arabic was slight although that was supposed to be the court language, complained that he was weary of hearing poems in his praise that he couldn't understand; a courtier obligingly produced a poem which he could understand, in Persian, and Persian poetry was reborn after what came to be called the "two centuries of silence."

The language of panegyric in effect became the language of poetry. When poems were written on other subjects they were written within the ethos of, and utilizing the vocabulary of, panegyric because this was seen to be the appropriate language for poetry. The speaker of a short or medium-length Persian poem usually addresses a *you*, like a courtier addressing his prince. The *you* is idealized vis-à-vis the speaker, who correspondingly humbles himself; the *you* is capricious and can withdraw its favor. Such a withdrawal is the worst thing that can happen to the speaker, who complains of the *you*'s cruelty and of the pains of separation; or the *you* can grant audience to the speaker and nothing can be more blissful for him. If the poem refers to a third person, a *he* or a *she* rather than a *you*, the same conventions apply—the speaker places himself infinitely lower—in power, grace, social position, etc.—than the poem's subject. This system of conventions isn't only applied to the situation from which it arose, the prince/courtier relationship, but also to other human situations—erotic love for example, friendship, the worship of God, relations within the family. What began as a rhetoric belonging to a particular relationship of authority and service, between a prince and his subject, became the rhetoric of poetry in general, whatever situation the poem might be dealing with.

The poems show other characteristics typical of court poetry: there are rivals about who are keen to catch the king's ear (or, in the erotic equivalent, the belovèd's ear); there is much gossip, suspicion and backbiting; the courtly conventions, and the presence of rivals, mean that emotion must often be disguised. Anger can flare up at others' success, particularly when it's at the expense of one's own. On the positive side, there is a delight in wealth, elegance, precious stuffs, fine nuances of emotion, the heady pleasures of spring at court with its garden parties and open-air social gatherings. It's a claustrophobic, rather hot-house world in which refinement of emotional response is a consciously indulged pleasure, and in which power struggles, be they erotic or political, are never far from the surface. The poetry of the Scottish Chaucerians—especially Dunbar's, with its mixture of elegance, virtuosity, jealousy, salaciousness, fury and refinement—shows us a roughly equivalent world, as in its different way does the Japanese *Tale of Genji*, in which much the same elements are present. All three are medieval worlds whose prime realities are the power of the prince, the intrigues of courtiers, the maddeningly attractive and risky possibility of being Fortune's favorite for a while.

Perhaps the closest European equivalent for apprehending the social realities of what life in medieval Persian courts was like, for a poet or for anyone else, is to be found in the small, brilliant, and often fiercely competitive courts of late medieval and renaissance Italy. Different parts of Iran for much of the period covered by this book were ruled from different centers of power, and only two dynasties—the Seljuks in the 12th century and the Safavids in the 16th—managed to unite the country under a single rule, and even then not entirely. The nature of such provincial courts, competing for prestige, and for the poets who conferred prestige, produced a system of often munificent patronage; the poet's skill was highly valued and he could always go elsewhere if he felt insufficiently rewarded. This was similar to the situation as it existed in renaissance Italy, even if here visual artists often fared more spectacularly well under the system than did poets (though poets were given court posts as well, as Tasso was at the court of Ferrara). Of course such a system produced its losers as well as winners, and complaints that others are getting all the rich pickings are not uncommon. Also the extreme instability of such a life—one might well lose favor at any time and, even if one retained it, one's prince might well lose power at any time—certainly had its effect on the poems, which frequently complain of the fickleness of the world in general and of courts in particular.

The atmosphere of the Persian and Italian courts, apparently so different in basic cultural orientation, would seem to have been surprisingly similar, at least as it touched the courtiers themselves. If we consider Castiglione's requirements of a courtier, formulated for the court at Urbino in the early 16th century, they are not so far from the 10th-century Persian poet/courtier Aghaji's boasts of his skills (p. 35). Aghaji implies that he's an excellent horseman and bowman, that he can read prose (i.e. recite out loud to a group), recite/sing verse ("their graceful shaking their notes" as Herbert characterized it), write a good hand (calligraphy is an art that has always been much practiced and admired in Iran), play a musical instrument, gamble, hold his liquor well, and play chess. His poem is itself evidence that he can write verse when a suitable occasion arises. We may assume that these were the accomplishments required of a 10th-century Persian courtier (and the list is born out by one of the earliest and most attractive Persian Mirrors for Princes, the *Qabusnameh*, written for his son by an 11th-century prince). A man with such skills and interests would certainly not have been at all out of place at Castiglione's Urbino. And even *sprezzatura*, that aristocratic "diligent negligence" as Ben Jonson called it and which Castiglione so admired, also had its equivalent in the Persian courts. When Castiglione writes "[I] finde one rule that is most generall … and that is to use in everye thing a certain disgracing to cover art withall, and seeme whatsoever he doth and saith, to doe it without paine, and (as it were) not minding it … Therefore that may bee saide to be a verie arte, that appeareth not to be art … You may say then, how to shew arte; and such bent studie taketh away the grace of every thing," he could be echoing the 12th-century Ghaznavid court poet Mas'ud Sa'd (see p. 73):

Whatever skill you have
Don't try too hard while you're about it —
Too much thoughtful effort
Spoils your work and shows throughout it.

Naturally some Persian poets turned their back on all this, or, if they couldn't quite bring themselves to do that, they grumbled about it a great deal. But their poems that are contemptuous of this kind of life (Anvari's for example; see pp. 97–103) were written precisely with it in mind, not from another non-courtly viewpoint because one hardly, in literary terms, existed. They push against it, as it were, but don't walk away from it. In fact the epigrammatic short forms, particularly the *qat'eh* (literally, "fragment") were often used momentarily to subvert the conventions of life and poetry out of which they were written—poking fun rather than pleading, expressing disdain rather than supplication, offering an insult rather than a compliment. But of course the force of such a reversal of poetic expectations resides precisely in the fact that it is a reversal. The conventions are seen to be broken or reinterpreted, and this is the point of the poem; with no conventions there would be no point. A few poets, it is true, do seem to be able to walk free of the whole thing—Naser Khosrow is an example and Sa'di, in some of his poems, can be another (though he as much as anyone retains the conventions of court panegyric in his lyric love poetry).

Though Persian poetry began in the secular atmosphere of the provincial courts of eastern Iran during the 10th century, and though it began with the secular function of praising and entertaining a prince and his companions, it very quickly developed in a new direction, that of mysticism. Here one may imagine that the court ethos would be quickly shed. But in fact the language of extravagant praise, longing and compliment which had been developed as a tool for panegyric, and which had then been used for erotic poetry also, was eminently suitable for poems of religious devotion. The coincidence is not only one of rhetoric, but also of the social conditions within which the poems were produced. Groups of sufis (mystical adepts) were organized into a kind of court, with the sufi sheikh taking the place of a secular monarch; he had absolute power like the monarch, he could advance and degrade his acolytes as the monarch could, he was considered all but infallible and invested with a quasi-divine aura as the monarch was. Instead of writing a panegyric to a prince the sufi adept wrote one to his sheikh, and apart from a detail or two the results were often indistinguishable. The rhetoric of panegyric, often with ambiguously erotic overtones (is the addressee a prince or a belovèd or God?), was reinforced rather than diluted by its adoption as the language of mystical verse. A particular twist was given by the mystical poets' frequent claim that they had *become* the object of their longing, that their own reality had entirely disappeared, something in the manner of Emily Brontë's Catherine Earnshaw: "Nellie, I *am* Heathcliff!" Abu Sa'id Abul Khayr, Rumi and Eraqi often insist on their own lack of reality when face to face with the object of desire, whether this is God Himself or the divine beauty as manifested in an earthly messenger/representative/guide. Abu Sa'id for example declared, "For a long time I sought God (*haq*), sometimes I found Him, sometimes not; now I seek my self and do not find it, I have become all Him, and all (is) Him." Rumi after he had met the wandering dervish Shams-e Tabrizi who converted him to sufi mysticism, called his short poems "The *Divan* (collected poems) of Shams-e Tabrizi," rather than "The *Divan* of Rumi," because he claimed that his own reality had been replaced by that of Shams.

IN POEMS DEALING WITH secular love and desire this language of praise and supplication produced a kind of verse very similar in conventions, vocabulary, imagery and general ethos to that of the poetry of *amour courtois* of the middle ages in Europe. In beginning to read this poetry the European reader thus has a vague feeling that he knows what all this is generally about, that the landscape is not wholly unfamiliar. There are some differences though, and it's worth looking at a few of them for a moment or two, as they modify the ways we are able to read the poetry.

There is first of all the question of the kind of imagery involved, and the strategies by which it is used. The imagery of Persian court poetry can be very close to that of European medieval court poetry; in both, for example, images are often based on the rare and precious substances supposedly found at a court—jewels, precious metals, rare scents, fine cloths like silk and brocade—as if the whole poem were a subtle compliment to the audience's familiarity with such luxuries. The poem is presented as a little precious world, in which nothing vulgar or common can obtrude—even the grass is turned to emeralds and the dew to pearls—much as the court that is the poem's audience would perhaps like to see itself. Natural phenomena and such precious courtly substances are often compared to each other; a face is like silk, silk is like a petal, silver is like jasmine, jasmine is like pearls and so forth. Things in nature thought of as particularly beautiful—specific flowers and trees—as well as precious substances are both utilized in Persian poetry to describe the belovèd's body and face. This too, initially, seems close to European practice, both medieval and later ("My love is like a red, red rose"; "There is a garden in her face / Where roses and white lilies blow," "How silver-sweet sound lovers' tongues by night"); but because such comparisons in Persian verse very quickly became stylized they could be referred to as a generally understood code.

Here the convention differs from that of European poetry, and can make the poems particularly difficult to follow without some kind of gloss. Consider the following poem by the 12th-century poet Kafi of Hamadan:

> Last night the portion of that happiness
> Allotted in this world was given me;
> My bolster was of jasmine and I lay
> Pillowed on box-tree leaves: the moon and musk,
> Narcissi and the pomegranate flower,
> Silver, the cypress and the rose—till dawn
> Each of these seven was held in my embrace.

This makes no sense unless we know the code and, in its apparently disembodied and almost surreal images, seems closer in feeling to French *Symboliste* verse (by Pierre Louys say; one can imagine Reynaldo Hahn setting it) than anything from the European middle ages. But in fact the images are firmly anchored in a specific situation, it is simply that the tenor of each metaphor has been omitted (as if for example Luther were to write "A mighty fortress" without explicitly adding "is our God"). Jasmine is the belovèd's bosom, both for its colour (white) and its scent; boxtree leaves are her curls; the moon is her face (because of its radiance, not, as is often falsely assumed, because of its roundness); musk is her hair (again for its colour—black—and scent); narcissi are her eyes; the pomegranate flower is the delicate blush of her face; silver is the colour of her body; the cypress is her body's slender elegance, the rose is its softness, scent and complexion. The poem, then, is celebrating a night of erotic love; but its extreme delicacy of expression, the way it never actually refers to the body directly but only by recognized and elegant periphrases, the way passion is diverted into the compilation of what seems like a perfume maker's recipe, make it firstly a difficult poem for us simply to understand, till we know the code, and then, even when we have decoded the references, the way it expresses eroticism is distant from our expectations. European poetry has its Petrarchan periphrases to be sure, but is rarely so insistent about holding back from the slightest suggestion of gross sexuality.

Within its reticence and circumspection the poem is undoubtedly highly sensual—the colors, the contrasted black and white, the strong scents of musk and jasmine, the claim that this was the moment that encompassed all his earthly happiness, together give an unmistakable message of pleasure profoundly enjoyed. But the pleasure as it is communicated in the poem is enjoyed and savored as much as an aesthetic experience as a sensual one, and this deliberate and immediate aestheticizing of the moment underlines the poem's status as having been produced within an ethos of elegant connoisseurship. The specificity such a poem strives for is one of aesthetic nuance, and has nothing to do with the concrete particulars that generations of English schoolchildren have been taught to look for in poems. The act of aesthetic appreciation, of the aesthetic/ludic transformation of the moment, is as much the subject of the poem as the erotic encounter itself, which has all but disappeared as a physical reality. This seeking out of what one might call emotional connoisseurship is a distinctive feature of much Persian court verse (it was there from the beginning, though the effects did tend to become more *recherché* as time passed). Often what is offered is not reality direct, or the excitement that such reality might generate, but some special nuance of aesthetic effect that reality and its attendant excitements and anxieties can be called on to suggest.

A particular kind of trope, much used in Persian verse, also illustrates a basic difference in how material is often handled by Persian poets and their European equivalents. The trope's strategy is to describe an event or phenomenon or effect and then to ascribe an entirely fanciful cause to it, usually one that is by implication complimentary to the addressee (or, if one is writing that kind of poem, insulting to the addressee, though this latter is much rarer). For example in the poem on page 115 the 12th-century poet Tajaddin says that whenever he looks at his belovèd he weeps. So far so good, we are familiar enough with weeping lovers from our tradition. But then he ascribes the cause for his weeping; his belovèd is the sun (in splendor, uniqueness, beauty, power, etc.—all this is understood), and of course if you look at the sun your eyes water, so this is why he weeps. In the poem on page 87 the 11th/12th-century poet Atai Razi says that when he is away from his belovèd he can't sleep at night. Again so far so good, we have our sleepless lovers in poetry and reality alike. But the reason given is complex; his belovèd has sent Wakefulness to him as a messenger to keep him from sleeping. Why? Because if he falls asleep he might dream of embracing her. The complimentary references here are typically subtle; on the most basic level they indicate how obsessed he is with her (he can't sleep), but they also indicate the lovers' mutual concern (she sends the messenger, an act that seems both kind and unkind); concludingly, and the most delicate compliment together with the source of the poet's sorrow/complaint are to be found here, they indicate her modesty (no embraces, not even in dreams). Each line gives a slightly new twist, with the most delicate moment reserved for last.

This trope, the finding of fanciful complimentary causes for observable effects, is called in Persian *hosn-e ta'lil*, i.e. Beauty of Cause or Aetiology, and is a particularly prized poetic strategy. As with the habit of referring to things like jasmine and musk with the sure knowledge that your audience will interpret them as skin and hair, it was used from the beginning, but with greater elaboration and conscious sophistication as time went on. The trope hardly exists in English poetry: George Puttenham in his *The Art of English Poesie* (1589), perhaps the most comprehensive listing of the rhetorical strategies used in poetry to have appeared in English, does not mention it at all, although he lists over a hundred admirable "figures" and fourteen "vices and deformities." But, although it is rare in English poetry, examples of this trope can occasionally be found. There is a particularly clear example of *hosn-e ta'lil* near the opening of Milton's "On the Morning of Christ's Nativity":

> *It was the Winter wild,*
> *When the Hev'n born Child,*
>   *All meanly wrapt in the rude manger lies;*
> *Nature in awe to him*
> *Had doff't her gaudy trim,*
>   *With her great Master so to sympathize: ...*

In the last three lines of this stanza the bareness of Nature is described as being the result of Nature's awe before the Christ child, as if Nature were a servant baring its head before its master—a compliment exactly in the spirit of *hosn-e ta'lil*. The unreality and extravagance of the metaphor is validated by the (for Milton and his audience) miraculous nature of the poem's subject, the birth of the Saviour. The conventions of Persian poetry encourage a poet to employ this kind of "miraculous" imagery for the praise of mundane rulers and lovers, and this can at first sight appear egregious to Western taste, which even at its most Gongorist tends to be more empirical than its Persian counterpart.

I have been referring to the belovèd in the poems mentioned so far as *she/her*. There is no particular warrant for this (though in the case of Kafi of Hamadan's poem it seems likely that the belovèd is in fact meant to be taken as a woman). Persian pronouns have no gender or case distinction, so that the same word is used for *he/she/him/her*. There is no way of knowing, simply from the pronouns, whether the addressee/subject of the poems is to be taken as male or female. There may though be other indications; if there is a reference to pomegranates the poem is about a woman, as these are the normal periphrasis for breasts; if there is a reference to the new grass of spring the poem is to a young man, as this is a periphrasis for the first signs of an adolescent boy's beard. But often the reader simply has to guess—or not guess, the ambiguity being part of the point (a translator into English unfortunately often has to make a choice, usually a quite arbitrary one). Many of the poems are certainly to young men, homosexual liaisons being celebrated in various forms of Persian court art, including memoir, poetry and painting.

Interestingly enough it's possible to see a genre/sexual distinction operative in Persian poetry. Long narrative poems in Persian that deal with erotic subjects, and there are many of them, tell almost exclusively heterosexual stories. Long poems that are among other things anthologies of various shorter stories (like Attar's *Manteq alTayr* and his *Elahinameh*) often include anecdotes about homosexual relationships; but a love story which extends over the whole length of the poem, and whose telling is the final reason for the poem's existence, is virtually always a heterosexual narrative. Short and medium-length poems are on the other hand often overtly, or at least implicitly, homosexual. It is as if, within the culture, the homosexual relationship cannot be fully explored as a complete life-narrative, as if some residual taboo were still half operative, though it can be continually examined for its incidental and momentary emotional and epigrammatic effects. It's quite clear for example that Sa'di's erotic poems are, by and large, to adolescent young men (though he does have the occasional pomegranate breast peeping out here and there), as are the mystical poet Eraqi's. Many poets seem to celebrate liaisons with both sexes with equal enthusiasm; the very scabrous poet Obayd-e Zakani (perhaps the prime example in Persian of a poet who turned all the conventions upside down for shock effect) says it's all the same to him whether he finds a rent-boy or a female whore:

> *I'm off to stroll through the bazaar—and there*
> *I'll see what can be flushed out from its lair;*
> *I'll lure a rent-boy home here, or a whore;*
> *One of these two, either will do,* I *don't care!*

and, even if they put it more delicately, other poets seem to imply the same sentiment.

It is important too to remember the social context of the poems. They tended to be public entities, even when apparently about intimate matters. There are many stories about poets finding a place at court by being able to come up, in public, with an impromptu line of verse, or complete poem, at an apposite moment. The great 10th/11th-century epic poet Ferdowsi was said to have been admitted to the Ghaznavid court because he produced what seemed to be an impossible last rhyme for a quatrain (that the story is almost certainly apocryphal does not detract from what it indicates—that such ready skill was greatly admired). In this book the 12th-century woman poet Mahsati (also pronounced "Mahasti"—there is disagreement as to the correct form) is supposed to have been welcomed to the court of the Seljuk king, Sanjar, because she extemporized a quatrain in the king's hearing, when he was held up on a journey by a fall of snow, saying in effect that nature had decked itself out in silver in his honor. As it happens, the poem includes both of the rhetorical strategies indicated above as characteristic of medieval Persian epigrams—a natural phenomenon (snow) is compared to a precious substance (silver), and an observable effect (a snowfall) is given a fanciful and complimentary aetiology (nature is decking itself out in splendor to honor king Sanjar). A witty poetic retort was also greatly prized—the best known in this volume being the response of the poet Rashidi to criticism of his verse by his rival at court Ama'q (see p. 91), and many of the short poems of Anvari and Sa'di translated here read like off-the-cuff occasional pieces which were then thought witty enough to preserve.

MOST OF THE POEMS given here are of one of two kinds, called respectively *qat'eh* and *do-bayti*. The first, which as has been mentioned literally means "fragment," usually rhymes *abcb* (though it may be of more than four lines) and is normally used for witty, subversive, insulting or complaining poems. The second which literally means "two-liner" consists of what we would naturally call four lines rhyming *aaba*—occasionally *aaaa*; the two long lines have internal rhymes in Persian, so that the form is as follows:

$$(1) \underline{\hspace{2cm}} a \qquad (2) \underline{\hspace{2cm}} a$$
$$(3) \underline{\hspace{2cm}} b \qquad (4) \underline{\hspace{2cm}} a$$

The *rubai* (pl. *rubaiyat*), made famous in the west by Fitzgerald's translations of Khayyam, is a specific kind of *do-bayti* in a particular metre. *Do-bayti* and *rubaiyat* tend to be used for more "serious" poems, those in which the courtly conventions are celebrated rather than subverted (though this rule doesn't always hold) and very often the point of the poem, the knife that enters the heart, as the Persian phrase has it, is reserved for the last line and if possible for the last rhyme. A few of the poems given here, especially from the earlier poets, are literal fragments; that is, they are moments from longer poems that have been lost; usually the surviving moment has been preserved in a biographical notice on the poet or in a book of literary criticism/connoisseurship. A very few of the poems are excerpts from longer works that, due to their being anthologized in this form, have come to be regarded almost as complete poems in their own right (like, say, the boat-stealing incident from Wordsworth's *The Prelude*).

VERSE TRANSLATION IS something of a no-man's-land to work in, and as in any no-man's-land there are incoming shells from both sides. Scholars tend to look down on it because it's verse, with all the license that can imply, rather than a crib with footnotes; poets often disparage it because it's translation rather than original work. A word or two about how I have set about translating these poems, and why I have made some of the decisions I have, might be useful.

There is first the question, Why verse at all? Why not just produce plain prose cribs? The main answer to this objection is that such poems depend almost for their existence on the fact that they *are* poems; they don't tell a story or describe a landscape or give a psychological portrait—that is, they don't have a strong content which stands up as interesting when it's divorced from the poetic form. In this they are like Sappho's poems, or the songs of Campion and the anonymous writers who provided words for the Elizabethan madrigalists. If one takes away the form the poem has virtually dissolved, only a slight and often not very interesting residue is left. To translate such works means to take full account of their form, because it's here that their reality largely resides, and to try to find some kind of verbal equivalent for it in one's own language.

There is also the feeling that such treatment may be all very well for works that are well-known, but if one is translating hitherto untranslated works—as virtually all the poems in this anthology are—then isn't it best just to give the plain meaning? We can have infinite versions of Horace because there are in fact so many versions already, and there is always the Loeb to look at as a crib. But this is to ignore the fact that almost all the great poetical works that have been translated into English have received their first translations, when no Loeb or any other corroboration existed, precisely into verse. One need only cite Gavin Douglas's *Aeneid*, Chapman's Homer, Harington's Ariosto, Fairfax's Tasso. In each case the fact that a poem was being translated meant that the translator felt that, if he were not wholly to betray his author, he had, naturally, to produce a poem in English.

Related to this is the question of why translate into strict form, when surely one can approach the original meaning more closely in free verse? There are two answers to this. The first is similar to my answer to the question, Why not prose? The formality of these poems as they exist in Persian is part of their reality; they need some corresponding formality in English if anything of their ethos is to be brought across.

The second answer is that although in theory one might approach closer to an author's meaning in free verse, it's rarely so in practice. Indeed translations into free verse from Persian poetry by and large deviate much further in sense from their originals than do translations into strict verse, difficult to believe as this might appear to be. For example Basil Bunting's few translations from Persian into relatively strict form (i.e. with rhyme and metre), available in his *Uncollected Poems*, are in general far closer in both spirit and literal accuracy to their Persian originals than are the free verse versions he included in his *Collected Poems*. This is not necessarily a criticism of Bunting; he did know Persian and was aware of what he was doing when he deviated from the sense of the original, and though his model as translator was obviously Pound. Vikram Seth's cogent characterization of Pound's Chinese translations "compounded as they are of ignorance of Chinese and valiant self-indulgence"[1] cannot be used to describe Bunting's Persian translations, at least as far as the ignorance goes. In his free verse versions Bunting was using the Persian largely as a starting point from which to write his own poems; the greater fidelity of his metrical, rhymed translations does, I think, nail the fiction that free verse is likely to be more faithful to the original author's meaning. It may be that

---

1   Vikram Seth, *Three Chinese Poets*, London, 1992, p. xxv.

there is some psychological law of analogy involved here. The translator into strict verse is used to working within limits, and he accepts as a crucial limit his author's apparent meaning. The writer of free verse is used to transgressing limits, to writing *against* rather than within a set of existing rules, and as often as not he's not going to let another limit, like what someone else seems to have meant, get in his way.

My own practice has been to try to find a formal equivalent in English for what is happening in the Persian. To this end I have set myself certain rules, the main two of which are that no images are added (all the images in the translations are in the originals, certainly by implication and usually quite literally), and that the poem should be at least something like the original as regards its form. As I translated more of these poems it became easier to keep to these formal requirements. A few of the first of the poems I worked on (for example some by Mas'ud Sa'd) consequently look, formally, more like English poems than Persian ones; but even here a recognizable relationship is present.

In general I have tried to translate poems keeping the same rhyme scheme, keeping the point of the poem in the same place (usually the last line), and doing my best to reproduce what I take to be the original's tone. Inevitably some compromises have been made. For some poems that rhyme *aaba* in Persian I have resorted to rhyming *aabb* or *abcb* in English (though most of the poems rhymed *abcb* here have the same rhyme scheme in Persian). I've very occasionally changed the order of phrases, and a couple of times the tenses of verbs in a poem. Some phrases are omitted because they would require a footnote to explain and the point of the poem seems to survive without them. Some Persian formal effects don't seem to work at all in English and I've abandoned them; some, though equally unfamiliar in English, seem to work quite well and I've adopted them where possible. For instance, many Persian poems rhyme three or four syllables before the end of the line; the last syllables of the line are then taken up with a phrase (called in Persian the *radif*) that is repeated each time the rhyme recurs. The poem by Sadr-e

Zanjani on page 169 provides a good example of this technique.[2] In general I have not tried to domesticate unfamiliar references by providing equivalents from our own culture, as for example was common practice in the 18th century—e.g. in Dr Johnson's versions of Juvenal (Tony Harrison's *Martial* is a brilliant modern equivalent). I've broken this rule a couple of times when it seemed the easiest way to convey a point, so that in one poem I write "Croesus" (a figure unknown to Persian mythology) to indicate someone fabulously rich, and in another I talk about "dollars" rather than "dinars" because it gave me a handy rhyme.

In undertaking such a project one finds many borderline cases and only tact can decide whether a version should be rejected because it strays too far from the original, or kept because it preserves enough of the original to make it worthwhile. Probably others in my position would find some of my inclusions too lax and some of my exclusions too severe. But my final vote has always gone according to whether the epigrammatic point of the poem has survived or not. Often the poems one most admires prove the most intractable and their English versions have to be abandoned. My biggest regret is the exclusion of a poem by the Indian poet Fayzi on the death of his child; the extreme beauty and simplicity of the verses make them appear easy to translate, but the task defeated me. There are many other poems that I had reluctantly to stop work on because I realized I was never going to get them to "speak English"—at least as many as survived and are included here.

---

2   As far as I'm aware one of very few English poets who occasionally use rhyme plus a short *radif* in this way, other than for comic effect, is Kipling ("I stayed the sun at noon to tell / My way across the *waste of it*; / I read the storm before it fell / And made the better *haste of it*"), presumably derived from his childhood familiarity with Urdu (Urdu verse utilizes the *radif* extensively). Kipling's general willingness to use feminine rhymes in serious poems, despite their association with comedy in English, may well come from the same source. The Dorset poet, William Barnes, was aware of the *radif* from his study of Persian, and he too experimented with it in a few poems.

Of course these are not cribs and are not meant to be, but neither are they simply my own poems based distantly on Persian originals. They are meant as examples of what Dryden, in his preface to *Ovid's Epistles, Translated by Several Hands*, called "paraphrase," eschewing the formless pedantry of "metaphrase" (a literal and necessarily amorphous word for word rendering) on the one hand and the license of "imitation" (using the original chiefly as an idea with which to write a poem of one's own) on the other. My aim has been to try to write within the long English tradition of verse translation, of which Dryden is one of the greatest practitioners; that is, producing competent verse in English which as far as possible does not betray the original. The versions offered here are, at the least, much closer to the Persian poems from which they derive than are Fitzgerald's brilliantly idiosyncratic versions of Khayyam (I have included nothing by Khayyam here, mainly in order to avoid comparisons). I have tried, though I am well aware of how far short of such a standard my translations fall, for something like Housman's achievement in his version of Horace's "Diffugere nives" ode: it's accurate within the limitations of verse, moving, clearly a translation but memorable in its own right.

Various friends and colleagues have given me encouragement and useful criticism during the five years or so in which I have been engaged on these translations. I should like to thank three in particular, Robert Barth, Wendy Cope and Timothy Steele. Robert Barth has an almost unrivaled knowledge of the history of the verse epigram in English and has himself written fine verse translations of one of the west's great masters of the form, Martial. As a publisher he produced two chapbooks each containing a selection of the epigrams translated here, and he encouraged me to devote time and energy to this project. Wendy Cope was one of the first of my friends to show enthusiasm for these translations, and I am very grateful to her for her kindness and encouragement. Timothy Steele read through the completed manuscript and made many very useful suggestions. My chief debt, as always, is expressed in the book's dedication.

A Geographical and Historical Note

MEDIEVAL PERSIAN POETRY was first written in Khorasan, the northeastern province of Iran, much of which does not lie within the country's present borders, including as it does most of the area immediately north and south of the river Oxus. The reader will notice that Persian poets were active in other areas outside modern Iran's borders, most notably Afghanistan and northern India. In Afghanistan the Ghaznavid and Ghurid dynasties were both assiduous supporters of Persian culture; the Ghaznavids also controlled much of northern India, and later the Moghul emperors ruling from Agra, Delhi and Fatehpur Sikri used Persian as their court language and encouraged the writing of Persian verse. Indeed by the end of the period covered by this book more verse in Persian was probably being produced in northern India than in Persia itself.

The following is a list of the dynasties mentioned in the biographical notes to individual poets:

Samanids

Prominent in Khorasan from the beginning of the 9th century. Ruled there from 875 until 999. The most important of the local dynasties which revived Persian culture after the Arab conquest of the 7th century.

Qarakhanids

Rivals of the Samanids in the area north of the Oxus during the late 10th century. A combination of Ghaznavid attacks from the southeast and Qarakhanid attacks from the northeast resulted in the Samanids' downfall.

Ghaznavids

A Turkish dynasty from central Asia, founded by former clients of the Samanids. Ruled in Afghanistan from 977 (where their capital was situated, at Ghazni, between Kandahar and Kabul). They conquered much of northern India and ruled in eastern Iran from 1005 till 1040. After being replaced in Iran by the Seljuks they continued to rule in Afghanistan and northern India for another century.

Ghurids

A dynasty from Afghanistan, prominent in the 11th–12th centuries; allies and rivals of the Ghaznavids, whom they briefly replaced as the chief power in Afghanistan and northern India during the late 12th century.

Seljuks

Like the Ghaznavids originally a central Asian Turkish dynasty. They entered Iran from the northeast during the 1020s and 1030s and controlled most of the country and much of the rest of Islamic southwest Asia by the 1050s. Ruled Iran till the death of king Sanjar in 1157.

Kharazmshahs

A dynasty ruling during the 11th, 12th and early 13th centuries in Kharazm ('Chorasmia'), the area of the lower Oxus where it entered the Aral Sea. Originally breakaway clients of the Seljuks, they replaced the Seljuks as rulers of much of northern and eastern Iran after the death of Sanjar. The dynasty was destroyed by the Mongol invasion of the 1220s.

Mongols

Iran suffered two Mongol invasions, under Genghiz Khan during the 1220s and under Timur the lame (Tamburlaine) during the 1380s. The wholesale destruction of towns, agriculture, populations and the infrastructure of civilization that occurred during these invasions, particularly the first, is one of the most horrifying chapters of world history.

Safavids

The most splendid of Iran's Islamic dynasties, ruling from 1501 until the mid-18th century when their power was destroyed by an Afghan invasion and a subsequent lengthy civil war.

Moghuls

The dynasty founded by Babur, a descendant of Tamburlaine, which ruled in north India from the 1520s. The court language was Persian and under the patronage of the Moghul emperors a distinctive Indo-Persian culture of great sophistication and elegance grew up. The last Moghul emperor, whose power was by this time largely titular, was not deposed by the British until after the Great Rebellion (which we used to call the Indian Mutiny) of 1857.

A Note on the Text

The texts for the poems translated here are taken from the following books:

Ganj-e Sokhan, ed. Zabihollah Safa, 3 vols., Tehran, n.d.

Tarikh-e Adabiyat dar Iran, ed. Zabihollah Safa, 5 vols., Tehran, reprinted 1366/1987

Hezar Sal She'r-e Parsi, ed. Ja'far Ebrahimi *et al.*, Tehran, 1365/1986

Nozhat al-Majales, ed. Mohammad Amin Riahi, Tehran, 1366/1987

Pishahangan-e She'r-e Parsi, ed. Mohammad Dabirsiaqi, Tehran 2536/1978

Kolliyat-e Eraqi, ed. Sa'id Nafisi, Tehran, n.d.

Divan-e Onsori-ye Balkhi, ed. Mohammad Dabirsiaqi, Tehran, 1363/1984

Sokhanan-e Manzoum-e Abu Sa'id Abul Khayr, ed. Sa'id Nafisi, Tehran, n.d.

Kolliyat-e Sa'di, ed. Mohammad Ali Foroughi *et al.*, Tehran, n.d.

Kolliyat-e Obayd-e Zakani, ed. Parviz Atabeki, Tehran, 1343/1964

Divan-e Qatran-e Tabriz, ed. Hasan Taqizadeh et al., Tehran, 1362/1983

Divan-e Anvari, ed. Sa'id Nafisi, Tehran, 1364/1985

Kolliyat-e Divan-e Shams-e Tabrizi, ed. Badi'alzaman Forouzan-far *et al.*, Tehran, 1351/1972

Divan-e Vahshi-ye Bafeghi, ed. Hosayn Nakha'i, Tehran, 1366/1987

Divan-e Mas'ud-e Sa'd, 2 vols., ed. Mehdi Nuryan, Esfahan, 1365/1986

Divan-e Kh'ajeh Hafez-e Shirazi, ed. Seyyed Abu'l Qasem Anjavi-Shirazi, Tehran, 1346/1967.

In preparing the brief notes on individual poets my chief debt is to Dr. Zabihollah Safa's *Tarikh-e Adabiyat dar Iran* ('History of Literature in Iran', 5 vols., Tehran, reprinted 1366/1987). I have also made use of Dr. Mohammad Amin Riahi's introduction to his edition of the 14th-century anthology of *rubaiyat*, the *Nozhat al-Majales* ("Pleasure of the Assemblies"), as well as using material from other sources.

آغازی بخداپایی

به هوا در نگار که لشکر برف
چون کند اندر او همی پرواز

راست همچون کبوتران سفید
راه گم کرده گان زیبت باز

اگر از دل حصار شاید کرد
جز دل من ترا حصار مباد

مهربانیت را شماری نیست
زندگانیت را شمار مباد

ای آنکه نداری خبری از هنر من
خواهی که بدانی که منم نعمت پرور؟

اسب و کمند آر و کتاب آر و کمان آر
شعر و قلم و ربط و شطرنج و می و نرد

AGHAJI

Born in Bokhara in modern Uzbekistan, Aghaji was active at the court of the 10th-century Samanid dynasty, which ruled in Khorasan (northeast Iran and much of what is now Uzbekistan, Turkmenistan and Tajikistan). Their splendid and relatively brief-lived court (they remained in power for a little over a hundred years) was one of the most vigorous instigators of the revival of Persian culture after the "two centuries of silence" which followed on from the Arab conquest of the 7th century.

Look how snow's army hurries through the air
Like white doves scattering from a hawk in fear.

★

If one can make a fortress of the heart
May no heart be your fortress but my own —
And may your days there be as countless as
The countless kindnesses that you have shown.

★

You want proof I'm not just a pampered brat?
You've no idea of what it is I do?
Bring me a horse, a bow, a book, some poems,
A pen, a lute, dice, wine, a chess set too.

شهید بلخی

اگر غم را چو آتش دُود بودی
جهان تاریک بودی جاودانه

در این گیتی سراسر گر بگردی
خردمندی نیابی شادمانه

دانش و خواسته‌ست نرگس و گل
که به یک جای نشکفند به هم

هر که را دانش است خواسته نیست
وانکه را خواسته‌ست دانش کم

SHAHID

Born in Balkh, in Afghanistan. A 10th-century poet, very little of whose
work has survived, active at the Samanid court. There is a quatrain
ascribed to his contemporary Rudaki lamenting his death, which states
that the eyes might say one man has died, but wisdom would say more
than a thousand.

If sorrow flared like fire its smoke would rise
Darkening forever all the earth and skies;
Wander the world, but you will never find
One man who's happy and who's also wise.

★

Great wealth is a narcissus
    And wisdom is a rose;
Where one will bud and flourish
    The other never grows —
The wise man's never wealthy,
    How little Croesus knows!

رودکی

شاد زی با سیاه چشمان، شاد
که جهان نیست جز فسانه و باد

ز آمده شادمان بباید بود
وز گذشته نکرد باید یاد

من و آن جعد موی غالیه‌بوی
من و آن ماه روی حور نژاد

نیکبخت آن کسی که داد و بخورد
شوربخت آن که او نه خورد و نه داد

باد و ابر است این جهان فسوس
باده پیش آر، هرچه بادا باد

RUDAKI

This 10th-century poet, born in a village near Samarkand in Uzbekistan, is considered to be the first major poet of "modern" (i.e. post-7th century) Persian. He was the most prominent poet involved in the Samanid revival of Persian literature.

Live your life in happiness
    Live with girls whose black eyes gleam,
For the world is nothing more
    Than a wind-swept empty dream;
Do not fear what is to come
    Or remember what is gone —
I am here with her black curls
    And her face is like the moon;
Lucky he who dined and shared,
    Luckless he who did not dine —
Wind and cloud are all this world is,
    Let what must come, come: bring wine!

★

روی به محراب نهادن چه سود

دل به بخارا و بتان طراز

ایزد ما وسوسهٔ عاشقی

از تو پذیرد نپذیرد نماز

چون که نشینیم دو لب گشته فراز

از جان تهی این قالب فرسوده باز

بر بلبلیم نشین و می گوی به ناز

ای کشته ترا من و پشیمان شده باز

Where is the point in bowing down
       To Mecca when you pray
If pretty girls from Turkestan
       Have snatched your heart away?
God will accept the lures of love
       That led your mind astray,
But He will not accept the prayers
       You ritually pray.

★

That day you see me stretched out on my bed,
My mouth wide open and the spirit fled
From its exhausted mould—sit there and sigh
'I killed you, but I'm sorry you are dead.'

دقیقی

گویند صبر کن که ترا صبر بر دهد
    آری دهد ولیک به عمر دگر دهد
من عمر خویش را به صبوری گذاشتم
    عمر دگر بباید تا صبر بر دهد

DAQIQI

A 10th-century poet from Khorasan (Balkh, Samarkand and Tus—near
Mashhad—have all been suggested as his birthplace) who, like his older
contemporaries Shahid and Rudaki, worked as a Samanid court poet.
At various points in his surviving poems he indicates that he is a
Zoroastrian (i.e. an adherent of the pre-Islamic faith of Iran), though
some scholars have doubted the truth of this. He is most famous as the
author of about one thousand lines of the Persian national epic, the
Shahnameh, which was then completed by Ferdowsi after Daqiqi had
been murdered by a slave.

Wait! Patience is rewarded, so they say;
Well, yes—when Death has carted us away.
My life has been one patient long delay:
Rewards, it seems, must wait till Judgement Day.

سبحینک ترمذی

نیکو گل دو رنگ آنگه کن

در ست بزیر عقیق ساده

یا عاشق و معشوق روز خلوت

رخساره بر رخساره بنهاده

MANJIK

From Termez on the shores of the Oxus, he was active in the second half
of the 10th century which makes him one of the "second generation" of
Persian poets after the generation of the progenitors like Rudaki and
Shahid.

Look at this parti-colored flower,
An agate streak, a pearl-pale streak —
Two lovers who have crept away
And lie together, cheek to cheek.

خردانہ

چہار گونہ کس ازمن عاجز نہ نشستند
کز آن چہار بہ من ذرہ ای شفا نایَد

طبیب و زاہد و اختر شناس و افسنگر
بہ دارو و بہ دعا و بہ طالع و تعوید

KHOSRAVANI

A poet of the 10th century active at the Samanid court. Mohammad Abdah and the great epic poet Ferdowsi are both said to have used lines by Khosravani as a starting point for poems of their own (this being a recognized way for one poet to pay homage to another).

There are four kinds of men who'll get no fee from me
Since I've seen not a scrap of profit from their arts —
The doctors with their drugs, the pious with their prayers,
Magicians with their spells, stargazers with their charts.

مُهر عبده کاتب

گویند مرا : چـرا گریزی
از صحبت و کار اهـل دیوان

گویم : زیرا که هُوشیارم
دیوانه بود قـرین دیوان

MOHAMMAD ABDOH

A poet and scribe of the Qarakhanid court—though, if the poem given here is to be believed, he had a jaundiced view of court life. He was active at the end of the 10th century. Little of his poetry has survived.

They ask me why I run away
From all that courtiers do and say:
Because I'm clever, I retort —
And only idiots live at court.

کبابی

گل نمیبت پیام فرستاده از بهشت

مردم کریم ترشود اندر نسیم گل

ای گل فروش گل چه فروشی بجای سیم

وز گل عزیز تر چه ستانی بسیم گل؟

KESA'I

Born in Marv (now Mary) in Turkmenistan in 952, he wrote in praise of the Samanid rulers of Khorasan and outlived their downfall at the hands of the Ghaznavids who invaded the country from the east at the very end of the 10th century.

Flowers come as a gift
          sent down from Paradise
And in their presence man
          lives with a kinder heart —
O Flower-Seller selling
          flowers for silver, what
Will silver buy more lovely
          than that with which you part?

مرا به قدر داری

دعوت من که تو آن شکل و ترفت عاشق کناد

بر کی سنگین دلی مهربان چون خویشتن

تا بدانی درد عشق و داغ مهر و غم خوری

تا بجز اندر پی سعیم و بدانی قدر من

عشق او باز اندر آورد م به بند

کوشش بسیار نامد سودمند

عشق دریایی کرانه ناپدید

کی توان کردن شنا ای هوشمند

عشق را خواهی که تا پایان بری

بس که بپسندید باید ناپسند

زشت باید دید و انگارید خوب

زهر باید خورد و انگارید قند

توسنی کردم ندانستم همی

کز کشیدن تنگتر گردد کمند

RABE'EH QOZDARI

The first woman poet of Persian whose name, and some of whose works, have survived. She was born near Balkh in Afghanistan, probably during the latter part of the 10th century. In common with other female Persian poets, various legends grew up concerning unhappy love-affairs. She is not to be confused with the female mystic Rabe'eh who lived in the 8th century in Basra. The lines that close the second poem given here (from "see ugliness as beauty" to the end), also appear as a separate poem in the *Asrar al-Towhid*, a 12th-century work of hagiography describing anecdotes from the life of Abu Said Abu'l Khayr, where they are quoted as Abu Sa'id's response to the death of his son.

My hope's that God will make you fall in love
With someone cold and callous just like you
And that you'll realize my true value when
You're twisting in the torments I've been through.

★

His love has caught me once again —
I struggled fiercely, but in vain.
(Well, sobersides, explain to me
Just who can swim love's shoreless sea!
To reach love's goal you must accept
All you instinctively reject —
See ugliness as beauty, eat
Foul poison up and call it sweet.)
I jerked my head to work it loose,
Not knowing all this would produce
Was further tightenings of the noose.

اندر غزل خویش نهان خواهم گشتن

تا بر لب تو بوسه زنم چونش بخوانی

غره مشو بدانکه جهانت عزیز کرد

ای بس عزیز را که جهان کرد زو نخوا

ماراست این جهان مجاهجوی ماگیر

وز مارگیر مار بر آر و دشتی دمار

آهو مرحمت را بغالد بر خوید

عاشق معشوق را بباغ نغالید

ای تو مکن آنها بیار با فتوح را

کانت مکاکفت ازین سرای گلایید

باد بر آید شاخ بید شکفته

بر سر منخوار برگ گل بغتالید

AMAREH

Born in Marv (modern Mary, in Turkmenistan); active during the last years of Samanid rule and the opening years of the Ghaznavid dynasty's control of Khorasan—i.e. at the end of the 10th and beginning of the 11th centuries. There is a story that someone recited the first of the epigrams translated below in the hearing of the sufi sheikh Abu Sa'id Abul Khayr. Abu Sa'id asked the name of the poet, and on being told it was Amareh led his companions to Amareh's grave in order to pay their respects to his dust.

I'll hide within my poems as I write them
Hoping to kiss your lips as you recite them.

⋆

Because the world's done well by you
Don't think you have good cause to crow,
It's done well by so many men
And—in an instant—laid them low.

The world's a snake, and anyone
Who tries to profit from it's like
A man who handles snakes; one night
The snake will see its chance and strike.

⋆

The deer pursues its doe; a lover searches
    Through the orchard, hoping his belovèd's there:
Grief-stricken, come—bring wine again that frees you
    From this harsh world and all its carking care:
A wind has risen in the flowering willow
    Scattering its blossoms on the drinkers' hair.

ابوسعید ابی الخیر

از واقعه‌ای ترا خبر خواهم کرد
وآنرا بدو حرف مختصر خواهم کرد

با عشق تو در خاک نهان خواهم شد
با مهر تو سر ز خاک بر خواهم کرد

گر مرده بوم برآمده سالی بیست
چه پنداری که گورم از عشق تهیست

گر دست بخاک بر نهی کانجا کیست
آواز آید که حال معشوقم چیست

ABU SA'ID ABUL KHAYR

One of the first of the long line of Persian mystical poets. His dates are given as 967–1048, and he was born somewhere in north-eastern Khorasan, perhaps near Marv. He has often been credited, though inevitably some scholars dispute it, with being the first to introduce the style and vocabulary of passionate mysticism into Persian poetry. Like the later Khayyam he is a poet who attracted numerous imitators and almost certainly many (some commentators go so far as to say almost all) of the poems that have been ascribed to him are not by him. Virtually all the verse said to be by him is in the form of separate quatrains, with a distinctive 'folksy' and ecstatic flavor.

I'm going to tell You something that is true
And won't take more than two words to explain —
I'll lie beneath the earth still loving You
And with Your kindness I shall rise again.

★

If I've been dead for twenty years or so
And you, believing love gone long ago,
Should stir my dust and say, 'Whose grave is this?'
'How is my love?' will echo from below.

★

ای دل چو در آتش رگ جان کشیدت

بنمای بکس خرقهٔ خون آلودت

بنال چنانکه نشنوند آوازت

بسوز چنانکه بر نیاید دودت

فردا که به محشر اندر آید زن و مرد

وز بیم حساب و بیم ها گردد زرد

من حسن ترا بکف نهم پیش روم

گویم که حساب من از این باید کرد

His absence is the knife that cuts your throat?
Let no one glimpse the blood-stains on your coat;
Weep, but in weeping let no listener hear;
Burn, but in burning let no smoke appear.

★

For men and women soon the day draws near
When dreading Judgement they'll grow pale with fear;
Bravely I'll show your beauty then and say
'I must be judged on this, my life is here.'

ناصر خسرو

مرا یاریست چون تنها نشینم
سخنگوی ولی نی راز داری

همی گوید که هرگز نشنود خود
ندارد غم ولیکن غمگساری

یکی پشتش و صد رویی هستش
بخوبی هر یکی همچون بهاری

بپشتش برزنم دستی چو دانم
که بنشستست بر رویش غباری

سخن گوید بی آواز ولیکن
نگوید تا نیابد هوشیاری

بهر وقت از نخنها حکیمان
برویش بر بسینم یادگاری

نگوید تا برویش ننگرم من
بچون هر ز از خنای بادسای

بتاریکی سخن هرگز نگوید
چو با حشمت منتظر شهریاری

NASER KHOSROW

One of the most fascinating of Persian poets, he was born in Balkh in 1003 and died in 1088. During a pilgrimage to Mecca and a subsequent journey to the Fatimid stronghold of Egypt he was converted to Esmaili Shi'ism (professed by the Fatimids). As well as a large body of poetry he wrote philosophical/religious prose works and an entertaining and very informative Travel Diary, *Safarnameh*. Both his prose and poetry bear the strong impress of an enquiring, independent and highly intelligent mind. Though it is fairly typical of his work in its air of mysteriousness, the relatively off-the-cuff piece given here is in a more relaxed style than most of his poetry which is characterized mainly by a restless intellectuality.

A Riddle

I have a friend who, when I'm all alone,
Sits with me—and how intimate we've grown!
He talks, but what he says he never hears,
He is unfeeling, but he dries my tears.
He has one back, he has a hundred faces
As lovely as the spring in desert places
(Sometimes I thump him on the back—I must,
He gets half-smothered in thick, choking dust).
He talks, but soundlessly; he has to find
A clever man before he'll speak his mind.
Whenever I encounter him, his eyes
Recall the precepts of the good and wise,
And yet he's quiet till I look his way,
Unlike some fools who blather on all day.
In darkness he falls silent—which is right,
He is a Prince who glories in the Light.

[The answer is 'a book']

عنصری

آمد بر من که؟ یار. کی؟ وقت سحر
تشنده رگ که؟ خصم. خصمش که؟ پدر
دادمش دو بوسه. بر کجا؟ بر لب تر
لب مه؟ نه، چه بد؟ عقیق. چون بد؟ چو شکر

ONSORI

Said to have been born in Balkh in 1039, he is considered one of the finest early panegyrists in Persian. As well as praise poems and short epigrammatic pieces he wrote one of the first partially surviving verse romances in Persian (*Vameq and Ozra*). The poem given here is also ascribed to Rudaki, under whose name Basil Bunting has translated it.

Who came to me? She did. And when? At dawn.
Afraid of whom? An enemy. Who is … ? Her father.
I kissed her twice. Where? On the lips. The lips?
Say rubies rather. And they were? As sweet as sugar.

قطران تبریزی

فراز و نشیب است روی زمین

متاز ای برادر گشاده عنان

سخن نیک بر سنج و از دل بگوی

ره راست بشناس و بی غم بران

بِرَنج ار بکاهم نالم زغم

رخ ار ببرم نخواهم امان

چو کورست گیتی چه خیر از هنر

چو کرست گیتی چه سود از فغان

QATRAN

An 11th-century poet from Tabriz in Azerbaijan in northwestern Iran. He is the first significant Persian poet of this area, and one of the first from any area outside Khorasan and eastern Iran. His best known poem is a panegyric that includes a description of the effects of a major earthquake that struck Tabriz. Naser Khosrow has a rather patronizing reference to him in his *Safarnameh* (Travel Diary), in which he says he had to explain some Persian verses by Daqiqi and Manjik to Qatran as Qatran couldn't understand them, and that though he wrote quite good poetry he didn't speak Persian well. He died in 1072.

Brother, we ride through difficult terrain —
  don't spur your horse, ride with a slackened rein:
Weigh your words well, then speak them from the heart —
  choose the right road, treat hardship with disdain.
If Grief unmans me I shall not cry out,
  if Fate destroys me I shall not complain:
The world is blind, what use is Virtue here?
  The world is deaf, we cry to it in vain.

اندرقی

اگر چه ترکید انهار سیم و زر سازند
برای نرگس هم خاک نرگستان به
بغربت اندر اگر سیم و زر فراوان است
هنوز هم وطن خوش نشین مت و آخران به

AZRAQI

Azraqi was born in Herat in modern Afghanistan. He was active and apparently highly successful at the court of the Seljuk prince Toghan-shah, governor of Khorasan at the end of the 11th century. As well as panegyrics, and epigrams like the one translated here, Azraqi wrote narrative poems including a version of the Sinbad story.

What if the vases that they make to hold
Narcissi in are silver and pure gold?
The flowers grow better in the dirt and rain.

What if there's gold and silver beyond measure
In foreign parts? Home is the greater treasure —
For all its ugliness, and grief, and pain.

سنایی

گر آمدنم زمن بدے آمدمی

ورنیز شدن زمن بدے شدمی

به زین نبدے که اندرین دیرخراب

نه آمدمی نه بودمی نه شدمی

SANA'I

The first of the three major authors of long narrative mystical poems in Persian (the other two being Attar and Rumi), Sana'i was born in the second half of the 11th century and died in 1150. He was attached to the Ghaznavid court which despite its non-Persian origins (the founders of the dynasty were originally central Asian Turkish slaves) actively patronized Persian culture. The poem given here is also attributed to Omar Khayyam.

If I could choose to come, I'd not have come;
If I could choose to go, when would I go?
The best would be if I had never come,
And were not here, and did not have to go.

در باغ چه روشنی که در روی تو نیست
در خلد چه خرمی که در کوی تو نیست
مشک ختنی زلف خوشبوی تو نیست
کیمیا سری عبیر تو خربوی تو نیست

با همت بازباش و با کبر پلنگ
زیبا بکن کار و بپر و زی نهنگ
کم کن عندلیب و طاووس درنگ
کانجا همه پاک آمده اینجا همه رنگ

MAS'UD-E SA'D

Born in Lahore during the second half of the 11th century, Mas'ud Sa'd spent his adult life as a functionary of the Ghaznavid court, as his father had before him. He was twice imprisoned for lengthy periods (eight and ten years), apparently for intervening too strenuously in the political life of the time, and he is famous for the poems he wrote during his imprisonment. These are the most well-known of what became a whole sub-genre of Persian literature. The last four poems translated here refer to his imprisonment. After being released from his second period of imprisonment he ended his life as the royal librarian. He died in 1121. A "parasang" (in the sixth poem) is about three or four miles. The "iron" of the last line of "My word was law …" signifies iron fetters placed on the ankles.

The moonlight has no beauty
Which is not in your face;
The joys of being near you
Make where you are a place
To rival Paradise;
Fine musk cannot compare
With that bewitching scent
Which hovers in your hair;
You are a perfect creature
With just one fault—your nature.

★

Be as a hawk in your desire,
A leopard in your majesty —
Bring beauty to the hunting ground
And to your battles victory.
The peacock and the nightingale
You would do better to ignore —
One is a gorgeous empty show,
One's a nice noise, but nothing more.

میدانم چو روز روشن صنما

کاخر بروی تو ازبرم صنما

زیرا چو کسی قصد در بستن صنما

نتوان بستن ترا با آهن صنما

اندیشه مکن بکارها در بسیار

کاندیشه بسیار بپیچاند کار

کاری که برایت آید آسان بگذار

ورنتوانی بکار دانان بسپار

گیتی و فلک بکشتن من یازد

زان برمن و روز و شب همی غم یازد

انگشت گرم زدست می نگذارد

درمعرکه دست تو مبارز دارد

I always knew—it was as clear as day, my love —
That sooner, later, you would go away, my love,
Because when you decided you must leave, my love
Not even iron chains could make you stay, my love.

★

Whatever skill you have
Don't try too hard while you're about it —
Too much thoughtful effort
Spoils your work and shows throughout it.

Do what comes easily,
Negligently, without a plan —
And if you can't do something,
Just pass it on to those who can.

★

Heaven and earth connive to murder me —
They rain down sorrows day and night against me;
It's no surprise they will not let me be
When they can count on you to fight against me.

★

راز اول بمیان ما بهنگام کنار

گر تار قصب بودی بودی دشوار

اکنون بمیان ما دوای یک دل ماست

فرسنگ دویست گشت سنگ بار

در باغ هنر تخم وفا کاشت خرد

تن را بهوای خویش نگذاشت خرد

رنج از دل رنج دیده برداشت خرد

ناآمده را آمده پنداشت خرد

در دولت شاه چون قوی شد پایم

گفتم که رکاب از زر فرمایم

زر گفت مرا که من تراکی شایم

آمد آهن گرفت هر دو پایم

When we were friends at first you made a fuss
    If just one layer of linen lay between us;
Yet now my dear two hundred parasangs —
    A thousand—measure out the way between us.

     ★

In Virtue's garden seeds of Faithfulness are sown
                          by Wisdom,
And to its own desires the body's left alone
                          by Wisdom,
Sorrow in sorrow-stricken hearts is overthrown
                          by Wisdom,
And what is yet to come is seen as here, and known
                          by Wisdom.

     ★

My word was law at court, and with what pride
I said, 'I'll have gold stirrups when I ride'.
'I am not worthy of you' gold replied:
What gold refused my feet, iron supplied.

     ★

هر یک چندی به قلعه‌یی آرندم
اندر سنجی کنند و بسپارندم

شیرم که به دشت و بیشه بگذارندم
پیلم که به زنجیر گران دارندم

نی روزم هیزم است و نه شب روغن
زین هر دو بغر سوده مرا دیده و تن

در حبس شدم مهر و مه قانع من
کاین روزم گرم دار و آن شب روشن

They bring me to the palace every now and then
And make me crawl to them, and send me off again —
A lion they won't let near a thicket or the plain,
An elephant they goad and handle with a chain.

★

No kindling for the fire, no oil to give me light,
My body's now as faint as my uncertain sight —
But I'm a prisoner here and sun and moon content me,
One warms me through the day, one shines for me at night.

اشعری

ای دل همه روز در غمت میسپنم

وی دیده همیشه در رَهَت میسپنم

ای صبر که دی همیگفتیم آن

امروز کجایی؟ که کمت میسپنم

از تاب تو بوده در تب: این کیست منم

صد روز به غم کرده شب: این کیست منم

وین لحظه چنین به طرب: این کیست منم

در پیش تو زنده یا رب: این کیست منم

ASHHARI

Born in Nayshapour in the 12th century, Ashhari was a functionary at the court of the Kharazmshah dynasty, which ruled in northern Iran. Most of his poetry has been lost, though he had a great reputation in his day. 119 of his *rubaiyat* were included in the *Nozhat al-Majales*, which ensured their survival.

All day, my heart, you've been upset,
And you, my eyes, are always wet —
But Patience (yesterday you talked
So big!) you haven't turned up yet …

★

One burned and yearned for you with all his might:
                and who might that be? Me!
Grief turned a hundred of his days to night:
                and who might that be? Me!
One at this moment knows supreme delight:
                and who might that be? Me!
One lives, dear God, here, now and in your sight:
                and who might that be? Me!

بفرج رونی

ما یک نفس از حیات قانعیت مرا
در سر هوس شراب و ساقیست مرا

کاری که من اختیار کردم این بود
باقی همه کار اتفاقیست مرا

هر تیر که در جعبهٔ افلاک بود
آماجگهش این دل غمناک بود

با چرخ چنین ظالم و بی باک بود
آسوده کسی بود که در خاک بود

چو نیست که عشق دل از تن خیزد
رو بر دل و تن هزار شیون خیزد

آری چو ز رنگ همی آهن را
هر چند که زنگ هم ز آهن خیزد

BULFARAJ-E RUNI

Born in Lahore of Persian parents, he was attached to the Ghaznavid
court, and died probably early in the 12th century.

While I've one breath remaining I shall pine
For that young servant and his heady wine;
This is the part of life I've truly meant —
The rest came only as an accident.

★

The wretched target of each dart
In heaven's quiver is my heart;
While Fate's so harsh, no man sleeps sound
But he whose bed is underground.

★

How is it love arises from the heart
    And then torments the heart that bore it?
Just think of rust and iron; rust's born from iron —
    What does it do but gnaw it … gnaw it.

یه حسن غزلی

رفتیم و گرانی ز رخ صالت بردیم

در دیده نموده جمالت بردیم

تا مونس همره و یادگاری باشد

دل را بربودادیم و خیالت بردیم

یکچند نهان سوی دلارام شدیم

واکنون به عیان حبت می و جام شدیم

رسیدن ماهمه ز بدنامی ماست

اکنون ز چه ترسیم که بد نام شدیم

SEYED HASAN-E GHAZNAVI

A poet active at the Ghaznavid court during the first half of the 12th century.

Weighed down by grief, I took the memory of
Your beauty with me when we had to part —
Because friends need mementoes of each other
I took your image, and I left my heart.

★

I used to look for pleasure cautiously,
Now I drink wine and don't care who comes near —
I was afraid I'd lose my reputation,
Now that I've lost it what is there to fear?

مُختاری

ز اول تو بدیدار زریرِ بودی

لیکن بی‌وفا عمر مرور بودی

چون در نگریستم نه در خور بودی

تو نیز نیازموده بهتر بودی

MOKHTARI

A poet active at the Ghaznavid court during the late 11th and early 12th centuries; a contemporary and colleague of Bulfaraj, Sana'i, Atai Razi and Mas'ud Sa'd.

You were gold at first glance—but O
Your life's a meretricious show;
I looked a second time and found
That you were best the first time round.

عطای سلندی

اندر سفر خیالت ای ماه ژرف من
تا روز بدی به هر شبی غم خورم من
بیداری را نگاشتی بر سر من
تا باز خیال تو بیاید بر من

ATAI RAZI

A poet at the Ghaznavid court during the late 11th and early 12th centuries, best known for his epic poetry. He was a contemporary of Mas'ud Sa'd, on whose death he is said to have written a fine elegy.

Each night, as I was travelling, in each place,
I saw till dawn's first light your haunting face —
But you had sent me Wakefulness for fear
That in my dreams of you we might embrace.

عمعق

خواهم همه راکو زر عشق برو ت
تا من نگویم بس بخ نیکویت
یا خود خواهم همی دو چشم خود کور
تا دیدن دیگری نبینم سویت

AM'AQ

Born in Bokhara and active during the 12th century. He was given the title of Poet Laureate (*Amir al-Sho'ara*) at the court of prince Khezrkhan ebn Ebrahim who ruled in Transoxiana and was a generous patron of literature. Despite his supposedly prolific output, much of which is now lost, Am'aq is chiefly remembered for his quarrel with Rashidi.

Love makes me wish that everyone were blind
And only I could see you and revere you,
Or that my own two eyes were blind—and then
I would not see the others hovering near you.

رشیدی

شعرهای مرا به بی نمکی
عیب کردی: روا بود شاید
شعر من همچو شکر و شهد است
و ندرین دو نمک نکو نباید
شلغم و با قلیت گفتهٔ تو
نمک ای قلمبان ترا باید

RASHIDI

Born in Samarkand, and active at the same court as Am'aq. When their patron, Prince Khezrkhan, asked Am'aq what he thought of Rashidi's verse he replied that, while correct, it "lacked salt" (i.e. was somewhat insipid). Rashidi's vituperative response is given below. Khezrkhan is said to have been so tickled by Rashidi's poem that he gave the poet a thousand gold dinars which were then set out on trays for the court's admiration.

To Am'aq

You say my verse lacks salt—perhaps it's true,
My verse is sweet as sugar-cane and honey
And salt should not be added to these two.
Look, pimp—salt's good for beans and turnip stew,
The kind of muck served up as verse by you.

فخرالدین مبارکشاه غوری

گفتم که بسوخت این دل دیوانه
داری خبر از واقعهٔ او یا نه
خندید که آخر چه خبر دارد شمع
از سوختن و فتادن پروانه

FAKHRADDIN MOBARAK SHAH

A 12th-century poet from Marvrud (in Afghanistan, between Herat and Balkh), active at the Ghurid court which ruled at this time in northern Afghanistan.

I said, 'Are you aware of how love's scorched
My crazy heart?' And smiling she replied,
'My dear—come on! What does the candle know
Of how a moth has blundered, shrivelled, died?'

سمایی

نه یار شبی بکوی من بیّاد
نه رو خبری بسوی من بیّاد

شرمم آید بروی او آورَن
اینچ ارغم او بروی من بیّاد

SAMA'I

Born in Marv, he was active during the reign of the Seljuk king of Persia Sanjar (ruled 1119–57).

At night he never comes to visit me
    And I have heard no news of him.
I am ashamed to bring before his face
    The griefs I've faced because of him.

اندرز

عشقی که همه عمر ربّاند اینت
دردی که ز من جان بستاند اینت
کاری که به کوشش چاره پذیرد اینت
وانشب که بروزم نماند اینت

خاطری چون آتش هست و زبانی همچو آب
فکرت تیز و ذکاء نیک و شعر بی خلل
ای دریغا نیست ممدوح و سزاوار مدیح
ای دریغا نیست معشوقی سزاوار غزل

ANVARI

Anvari, who spent his early life in Tus in Khorasan, was active during the 12th century, at the court of the Seljuk ruler Sultan Sanjar. He is best known for his brilliant (and often very abstrusely allusive) panegyrics. The epigrams translated here mostly show another side of him— witty, cantankerous and often exasperated with court life. His distinctive style, which can be both highly technical and *recherché* and very colloquial and direct, had many imitators. The "sleeves" mentioned in "You sent a message ..." are a reference to the fashion of wearing sleeves extremely long so that they covered the whole hand; this may be seen in miniatures of the period that are illustrative of court life.

This is the love that lasts a life-time through;
This is the pain that tears my soul in two;
This is the grief with no known remedy;
This is the night whose dawn I'll never see.

★

A fiery mind, and words like water flowing,
Honed wit, quick thoughts, fine verse—I've got all those;
But where's the patron worthy of my praise,
The girl who's worth the love-songs I compose?

★

گر آذر که صلتی نبخشد امیر

از بوستان کرو بسیار باشد

عطای او بو چون خسته کردن

که اندر عمر خود یکبار باشد

مرا پیام فرستی همی که پرسش تو

چو چشم دارم بر من سلام چون نکنی

کشند پای مرا من دون بلی شعرا

چو دست بخشش از آستین برون نکنی

دوش مهمان خواجه‌ای بودم

اینت نامردی و اینت سگی

دوش تا روز هر دو نغنودیم

او ز سیری و من ز گرسنگی

A Stingy Patron

Take what he gives you, even if it's paltry —
To this lord *paltry*'s quite a bit;
A gift from him's like being circumcised —
Once in a lifetime, and that's it!

★

You sent a message asking why I don't
Respond each time you deign to glance my way;
Well, poets tuck their toes beneath their cloaks
When sleeves hide hands that don't know how to pay.

★

Last night I was a great lord's guest,
A real son-of-a-bitch, a bastard;
Neither of us could sleep till morning —
He'd eaten too much, and I'd fasted!

★

شعر تر و خوب بنده گویم

انعام نصیب غیر باشد

این رسم نو آمد است امسال

ان شاء الله که خیر باشد

هر بلا یی کز آسمان آید

گرچه بر دیگری قضا باشد

بر زمین نارسیده میگوید

خانه انوری کجا باشد

گفتم ترا مدح در بها مدح من

خود کرده ام نذار د با کرد خویش بود

چون احتشام بو المرح گفتت

بدرگشتم آب تر در جای خویش بود

I write a nice fresh poem,
But X's is declared the prize one;
   This custom's new this year ...
Let's hope it proves to be a wise one.

   ★

Every disaster heaven sends
— Even the ones not meant for me —
As soon as they arrive on earth
Ask, 'Where's the house of Anvari?'

   ★

I wrote a panegyric on you—and I'm sorry.
   There's no point in these lays of one's own making;
My praise was like a wet dream—when I woke I found
   I'd spent spunk on a worthless undertaking.

   ★

من و شاعر و شش درزی چهار دبیر

اسیر و خوار ماندیم در کف دو سوار

دبیر و درزی و شاعر گلو چنگ کنند

اگر چهارده باشند اگر چهار هزار

Me, three other poets, six tailors and four clerks
Were captured by two horsemen—it was infamous …
But poets, clerks and tailors can't put up a fight —
Not if there are fourteen—or four thousand—of us!

دل کو که به نامه شرح غم آغازم
یا جان که ز درد با سخن پردازم
از بی‌دلی و بی‌خبری کاغذ کلک
می‌گیرم و می‌گریم و می‌اندازم

جانا تو ز دیده اشک بیهوده مبار
دلتنگی من بس است دل تنگ مدار
تو معشوقی گریستن کار تو نیست
کار من بیچاره به من بازگذار

MAHSATI

The most celebrated of all Persian woman poets. She was from Ganjeh (in what is now independent Azerbaijan), and is said to have had a scandalous affair with the local prayer-leader's son. Poems that purport to be her and her lover's poems to one another have survived. She was active, apparently as a courtier/scribe, at the court of the Seljuk monarch Sanjar (1119–57). Though it's risky to try to discover autobiographical traits in this kind of verse, she does come over in her surviving work as a very witty and passionate free spirit. She was highly successful as a poet, and won the praise of her contemporaries and successors (the Safavid poets of the 16th century particularly admired her) to the extent that her style was widely imitated and given a special name—the "set-the-Town-in-an-Uproar" style.

I wish I had the heart
             to write a letter and complain;
I wish I had the soul
             to find the right words for my pain —
I'm so distracted, crazed
             with wretchedness, I pick my pen
And paper up ... and start to cry ...
             and throw them down again ...

        ★

Dear, dry your pointless tears, tears don't suit you —
I'm sad enough, you needn't be sad too;
Look, you're the loved one, crying's not your rôle —
Let *me* do what the lover has to do!

سودازده جمال تو بازآمد

تشنه شده وصال تو بازآمد

نوکن نفس و لطف تو بپش

کان مرغ شکسته بال تو بازآمد

کس چون تو به عقل زندگانی نکند

در شیوه عشق مهربانی نکند

ای یار سبکروح وصلت میش

شادم اگر این صبح گرانی نکند

آب ار چه بنیرد به جویم با تو

جز در ره مردمی نپویم با تو

گفتی که چه کرده ام، بگویی با من

آن چیست نکرده ای، چه گویم با تو؟

★

The one your beauty's overthrown
                    has come back home;
The one who thirsts for you alone
                    has come back home;
Prepare the cage again, scatter your seeds
                    of kindness there,
Look, broken-winged, the bird you own
                    has come back home.

★

You're no great intellect, and men like you don't know
The usual kindnesses a lover ought to show —
My flighty friend, I'm glad I'm with you here tonight,
I hope I don't regret it in the morning though …

★

Although we don't get on in any way
I'll be polite to you still, come what may.
'What have I done?' you ask. Just tell me what
You haven't done! My dear, what *can* I say?

صابر

چون بادل تهمت و فنا در یکت پوست
در چشم تو کیرنگ بود دشمن و دوست
بس بس که شکایت تو ما کرده به هست
رو رو که حکایت تو ناگفته بهوست

قدر مردم سفر پدید کند
خانه خویش مرد را بندست
تا بسنگ اندرون بود گوهر
کس ندانستمش قیمتش چند است

SABER

Born in Termez in Uzbekistan, he was for a while a poet at the court of
Sanjar (1119–57) where he was a friend and rival of Anvari. He is said
to have been deliberately drowned in the Oxus by the Kharazmid king
Atsez who suspected him of spying for Sanjar.

Your heart's devoid of loyalty, and so
Your eyes cannot distinguish friend from foe.
Enough, enough—it's better not to scold;
Your story isn't worth the telling. Go.

*

A man must travel if we are to know him,
His own house hems him in and doesn't show him;
No one can truly estimate the worth
Of gems still locked in stone beneath the earth.

واسع جبلی

گفتار لطیف و خوی نیکوست ترا

خوبی و لطافت صفت و خوست ترا

عیب تو جز این نیست که در عاشقی است

بیگانه و خویش و دشمن و دوست ترا

VASE'I JABALI

A poet of the 12th century (he died in 1160) who wrote panegyrics at the courts of the Kharazmid and Ghurid dynasties, as well as at the two major courts of the time—the Ghaznavid, and its chief rival, that of the Seljuk king Sanjar.

You're eloquent and have exquisite tastes,
Your character is kind and generous too;
Your only fault is that in love your friends
And enemies are all the same to you.

رفیع مروزی

چندین چه کنی ناز که تا چشم کنی باز
از عشق من و حسن تو آثار نماند

آزار مکن پیشه و بازار مکن تیز
کاین تیزی بازار تو بسیار نماند

RAFI' MARVAZI

A minor poet of whom almost nothing is known, though his name implies he was from Marv in Turkmenistan. On the basis of his poems' style he has been tentatively placed in the period of Seljuk rule in Iran (1037–1157) or perhaps a little later.

Why tease me? In the twinkling of an eye
Your beauty and my love will both be gone.
Don't set your price extortionately high,
You'll see it plummet—and before too long.

تاج الدین باخرزی

چو روی خوب ترا بیند این دو چشم رهی
بر آب گردد گویی هَمی سحاب شود

که هست روی تو خورشید و هر که در خورشید
نگه کند بزمان چشم او پر آب شود

TAJADDIN BAKHARZI

A poet of the Seljuk period, from the area of Bakharz in eastern Iran,
near the present border with Afghanistan.

Glimpsing your lovely face, my poor eyes stare
And brim with water like spring clouds; but there —
You are the sun; the eyes of anyone
Will water if he gazes at the sun.

جمال الدین اصفهانی

یک شهر همی کنند فریاد و نفیر
درمانده به دست زلف آن کافر اسیر

ای دل اگر از سنگ‌تنی می‌پذیر
وای دیده اگر که زنده‌ای عبرت‌گیر

دوستی گفت صبر کن زیرا
صبر کار تو خوب زود کند

آب رفته به جوی باز آرد
کارها به از آنچه بود کند

گفتم آب رفته باز آید
ماهی مرده را چه سود کند

JAMALADDIN ESFAHANI

A poet of the 12th century from Esfahan. As well as living by his poetry
he claims to have been 'in spring a painter, in the autumn a goldsmith'.
A remarkable poem by him contains a long and very graphic descrip-
tion of a famine in Esfahan: 'When human nature changed, and men's
behavior too / When decency and kindness disappeared / ... When
mothers ate their young like cats / ... When men would quarrel with a
donkey over hay / While others fought with dogs for bones / And ten
days in a row the corpses were laid out in tens / Along the main road of
the city and at the corner of each alley'. He was the father of the poet
Kamaladdin Esmail. In his poem on the famine he mentions the water
drying up in the stream beds and the fish dying as a result, and the
metaphor of the second poem given here may be a memory of this.

A whole town cries out in pain and despair
Caught in the curls of that infidel's hair:
My heart, if you're not made of stone, take care!
My eyes, if you're not blind, be warned, beware!

    ★

'Patience will solve your problems soon enough,'
    My good friend said:
'Things will improve, fresh water will refill
    The stream's dry bed.'
'What use will water be'—I asked him—'to
    A fish that's dead?'

شرف الدین شفروا

کس در عشق این همه استاد که من؟

یا از تو بدین درد دل افتاد که من؟

آنرا که میان ما جدائی افکند

دشنام مبادم چنان باد که من

SHARAFADDIN SHAFRAVA

A 12th-century Esfahani poet, most of whose poems were written in
praise of Seljuk princes.

Who has remained so long outside love's door, like me?
And suffered in his heart your scorn before, like me?
I do not curse the man who came between us,
I only wish him to be more—and more—like me.

عماری

دردی که مرا زان رخ نیکو ست ببین
وین خسته دل که بستهٔ اوست ببین
ای دشمن اگر بکام خویشم خواهی
برخیز و بیا و کردهٔ دوست ببین

EMADI

A 12th-century poet from Ghazni who worked for Seljuk patrons. The 14th-century anthology, the *Nozhat al-Majales*, gives the poem translated here to another poet, Sadr.

Look what grief that lovely face has taught me,
What weariness of soul its love has wrought me —
My enemies, to see me as you'd wish,
Just look to what a pass my friend has brought me!

شطرنجی

عمر دراز اگرچه زهر نعمتی نه‌بست
بی نعماک عمر دراز است دریغ

اندر دنیا زعمر درازای برادران
عمر دراز نیست که جان کند دراز

مثل آنکه او بود حسق
مردمان فیلسوف دانش‌ش

مثل سگ بود که باشد کور
مردمان جان و چشم خوانند‌ش

SHATRANJI

Born in or near Samarkand and active in Transoxiana at the end of the 12th century. The word *shatranj* means chess and it's probable that his name means "the chess player," a name attested elsewhere for courtiers, as chess was clearly a popular game at medieval Persian courts. But the word also means a kind of checkered cloth, perhaps because it could be used as, or looked like, a chess board, and the poet's name may possibly have had the more mundane meaning of someone who made or dealt in this kind of cloth.

It's true a long life is the best of riches
But, without riches, it's a life of sighing.
My friends, a long life spent in want is not
A life so much as an extended dying.

★

He is an idiot—and men
Call him a wise philosopher;
He is the apple of their eye —
What is he, though? A sightless cur.

★

علم از استاد به حاصل کن کار زوی کتاب

نتوانی نقطهٔ علم به حاصل کردن

همچو مرغی که خروسش بونخایه کند

چو زه نتواند از آن خایه برون آوردن

جمال مجلس باشد به مردم دانا

وگرچه باشد جامی نشست پاکش

چنانکه زینت هر بیت رفته است

اگرچه پایگه بیت به هست جاگیش

To learn, you need a teacher—one who knows.
You think that books alone will do the trick?
You're like a hen untrodden by the rooster —
Nice eggs, but they won't hatch a single chick.

★

A man outranked by everyone can speak
So wisely that it's his words we commend —
The beauty of a verse is in its rhyme
Though rhymes are always tagged on at the end.

خافقين

ای گوهر گم بوده کجا جویمت
پای آبله در کوی بلا جویمت
از هر هوس یکان یکان بریمت
ور نهر وطنی جدا جدا جویمت

KHAGHANI

Born in Shirvan in northern Iran. He is perhaps the most admired panegyrist of Persian poetry. His poem on the ruins of Ctesiphon, the seat of the pre-Islamic kings of Iran, is one of the most celebrated works in the language; it was once learnt by heart by virtually all Iranian children at some time in their school lives. Khaghani's mother was said to have been a Christian servant or slave from 'Rum', i.e. Byzantium. His normal style is highly allusive, concentrated and difficult, and the quatrain given here—though not untypical of his shorter pieces—is quite unlike the intellectually demanding poems on which his reputation mainly rests. His style strongly influenced that of subsequent panegyrists. He died in 1198.

My dear, lost jewel—with blistered feet
I'll search for you through sorrow's street,
Ask news of you in every land
From every voice I chance to meet.

مجيبه بلقيسى

یک دست مصحف و دگر دست بجام

گه نزد حلال مانده گه نزد حرام

ماییم در این عالم ناپخته خام

نه کافر مطلق نه مسلمان تمام

MOJIR BEYLAQANI

A 12th-century poet from Azerbaijan. He was a pupil of Khaghani and
wrote poems in praise of the Seljuks.

In one hand we've the scriptures, and in the other wine —
Now with what our faith approves, now with what's unclean;
And so we live our lives out, neither cooked nor raw,
Not all heathen, not quite Muslim, dithering in between.

ظهیر فاریابی

چون نیست در این زمانه عهد شکن
یک دوست که عاقبت نگردد دشمن

تنهایی را کنون نها دم گردن
با خویشتن خوش است زین پس من و من

ZAHIR FARYABI

A 12th-century poet born in Khorasan. He worked in Esfahan, where he served the Khojand family (see Sadr-e Khojandi, p. 135) and later in Azerbaijan. He died in Tabriz in 1201.

Since I've no friend in this dead, faithless time
Who doesn't prove to be my enemy,
I choose to be alone—*there's* happiness;
From this point on it's me and only me!

سیف الدین باخرزی

امروز که دستگاه داری و توان

بخشی که بر سعادت آرد بنشان

پیش از تو از آن دیگران بود جهان

بعد از تو از آن دیگران باشد هان

سیفا زجفای دهر بسیار منال

هرگز مکن از زمانه اظهار ملال

کاین دولت دیگران و این محنت تو

چون نیک نگه کنی خیالست خیال

هر چند کنی زعشق بیگانه شوم

با عافیت آشنا و همخانه شوم

ناگاه پری رخی به من برگذرد

برگردم از آن حیله و دیوانه شوم

SEYFADDIN BAKHARZI

A sufi sheikh from Bakharz in eastern Iran, he was active at the end of the 12th and beginning of the 13th centuries.

Now that you're able to, plant deep the root
Whose branches bear good-fortune as their fruit;
The world belonged to others before you,
And there'll be others when you've left here too.

★

Seyf, don't complain of how unjust life is
Or rage against existence and blaspheme,
Saying, 'so little's mine, so much is his';
See life for what it is—a dream, a dream.

★

However often I give up on love
And live again with Health and Common Sense,
Some pretty face will pass me by and then
Lunacy makes short work of Abstinence.

صمد رخجندی

آن عهد و فا که مینمودی، این بود؟

خود را به وفا همی ستودی، این بود؟

نه گفته بدی کام دلت خواهم داد؟

آن کام دلم که گفته بودی، این بود؟

SADR-E KHOJANDI

A member of an Esfahani family that held powerful positions in the town's religious establishment during the 12th and 13th centuries.

Those promises of loyalty you gave —
    is this what you meant?
Those boasts of being my 'devoted slave' —
    is this what you meant?
Didn't you pledge me the one thing I crave?
    is this what you meant?
Is this what I crave? The way you behave?
    is this what you meant?

دختر تالار

چند انکه به کار خویش وامیبنم

خود را به غم تو مبتلا میبنم

وین طرفه که در آینهٔ دل شب و روز

من مینگرم ولی تو را میبنم

THE DAUGHTER OF SALAR

A poet of the early 13th century. She lived in Mosul (in Iraq) and in Qonya (in Turkey) and achieved considerable success, despite the fact that not even her name has come down to us. A panegyric she wrote received this encomium: "The daughter of Hesamaddin Salar sent to his Majesty from Mosul this panegyric, which outdoes the gentle breeze of spring in its graciousness and the waters of Paradise in its flowing limpidity. His Majesty gave instructions that she was to be paid a hundred dinars of red gold for every line. As there were 72 lines, 7,200 dinars were dispatched to Mosul ..."

The more I search myself the more I see
That longing for your love has ruined me;
I gaze into the mirror of my heart,
And though it's me who looks it's you I see.

عایشه سمرقندی

دوشم همه شب ای نعمت جانم شا [؟]

بدگویانت که روزشان نیک مبا [؟]

از عهد بدت حکایتی می‌کردند

وانگه چی؟ دلم نیز گواهی میدا [؟]

AYESHEH SAMARQANDI

A 13th-century woman poet from Samarkand.

My hated love, last night and all night too,
They, curse them, told me stories about you —
Their gossip was you break your promises;
And d'you know what?—my heart said, 'Yes, it's true'.

شمس سجاسی

برخیز که عاشقان به شب راز کنند

گِرد در و بام دوست پرواز کنند

هر در که بود جمله به شب دربندند

الا در عاشق که به شب باز کنند

گفتم صنما با دلم چه جانبیت

زلف توبگذر یا لبت هپیدانیست

نرم از سرِ ناز گفت در لحظه مرا

دل می‌طلبی؟ رو که دلت با ما نیست

SHAMS-E SOJASI

A poet from the first half of the 13th century, from Sojas, a small town near Hamadan in western Iran. The first of the quatrains given here is ascribed in some manuscripts to Abu Sa'id Abul Khayr. The "roofs" in this poem refer to the flat roofs of the Middle East; here people often sleep in the summer months, and in areas where the houses are close together it's sometimes possible to move from roof to roof without descending to the street. And of course they are an easy place of rendezvous.

Get up! At night the lover's secret rite
Is haunting roofs and doorways, out of sight —
In darkness every door but one's shut tight;
The lover's door swings open then, at night.

★

I said, 'I've lost my heart again, my dear —
Your hair's to blame? Your lips? It's not quite clear.'
Quickly, softly, she said, 'You want your heart?
I haven't got it. Go … get out of here!'

سعدی

دشمن اگر دوست شود چند بار
صاحب عقلش ننهارد بدوست

مار همانست بسیرت که هست
ورچه بصورت بدر آید ز پوست

هرگز بمال و جاه نگردد بزرگ نام
بدگوهری که خبث طبیعیش در سرست

قارون گرفتمت که شدی در توانگری
سگ نیز بقلاد زرین همان سگست

SA'DI

One of the four or five greatest of Persian poets, he achieved an immense reputation in his own lifetime and it has never been in serious danger of diminishing. He is admired both for the canny humour and humane generosity of his usual sentiments, and for the elegance and ease of his style. He was born early in the 13th century in Shiraz, in the central province of Fars, and died in the same town in 1292. He travelled widely, receiving his (largely theological) education in Baghdad and visiting Syria and the Hejaz. In his works he claims both to have been captured by European Christians (and later to have been ransomed), and to have travelled to India; both these claims are now considered to be poetic fictions. Though the quatrains given here are only a tiny fragment of his output, they illustrate some of his favorite themes—don't criticize others, tolerance is all very well but the leopard doesn't change its spots so be wary, boys are best, try to get along with the world rather than sulking or berating it.

An enemy who turns into a friend
Will not be thought a friend by those with brains —
A snake can slough its skin for all to see
But its essential character remains.

★

The nature of an evil person's in his blood
And greatness doesn't come with classy jobs and dollars —
I thought that now you're wealthy you'd be generous
But dogs are dogs still, even when they've golden collars.

★

گر سعیدی زبان دراز کند

که فلانی به فسق ممتاز است

فسق ما بی بیان یقین نشود

او به اقرار خویش غماز است

گر تو گویی که حرف عشق مگوی

این قدر حکم در زبانم هست

لیکن ار منع گریه خواهی کرد

دجله را پیش باز نتوان بست

خویشتن را علاج می نکنی

باری از عیب دیگران خاموش

محتسب کو ن برهنه در بازار

فتنه را میه مکن که روی بپوش

If some big blabber-mouth declares
    That so-and-so's philandering
We can't take talk like that on trust,
    So it's himself he's slandering.

★

If you should say to me 'Don't mention love'
I'll manage to restrain my tongue by force,
But if you try prohibiting my tears
The Tigris can't be altered in its course.

★

Until you can correct and heal yourself
Be quiet about another man's disgrace —
Don't be the bare-arsed bullying constable
Who hits a whore and tells her 'Veil your face!'

★

طبیب و تجربت سودی ندارد

چو خواهد رفت جان از جسم مردم

خر مرده نخواهد خاست بر پای

اگر گوشش بگیری خواجه و ردم

روزی نظرش بر من درویش آمد

دیدم که معلم بد اندیش آمد

نگذاشت که آفتاب بر من تابد

آن سایه گران چو ابر در پیش آمد

وقت گل و روز شادمانی آمد

آن شد که بر ما توانی آمد

رفت آنکه دلت بهر مکارم بود

سر ماند و وقت مهربانی آمد

When once the soul is ready to depart, sir,
All surgeons and their science are sure to fail,
Since no dead donkey's going to stand again
However hard you pull its ears or tail.

★

He glanced at me one day—but then his mean
Suspicious tutor had to intervene;
He wouldn't let the sunlight fall on me
But like a louring cloud pushed in between.

★

The time of flowers and every pleasant sight
                      has come,
The one thing that would never turn out right
                      has come —
Whatever made you disregard my love
                      has gone;
Now winter's gone, the season of delight
                      has come

★

درخت قناعت به آدم روزی چند

چشمم بدهان واعظ و گوش تن پند

ناگاه بدیدم آن سهی سرو بلند

وز یاد برفتم سخن دانشمند

در یک کرین جهان گذر خواهد بود

وین حال بصورت دگر خواهد بود

گر خود همه خلق زیر دستان تواند

دست ملک الموت زبر خواهد بود

هر روز بشیوه ای و لطفی دگری

چندانکه نگه میکنمت خوبتری

گفتم که بقاضی برمت از دل خویش

بستانم و ترسم دل قاضی ببری

O I repented, wore my pious cloak,
Listened and looked wherever wise men spoke,
But then I saw that cypress-bodied boy
And I forgot their sayings at a stroke …

★

Learn that one has to leave the world one day,
That how things are is not how they will stay —
If one man now has all men as his subjects
It is King Death whose hand he must obey.

★

Each new day you come up with something new,
You're lovelier every time I look at you;
I said, 'I'll take you to the judge and get
My heart back.' But I'm afraid you'll steal his too.

شهاب کاغذی

لطفی بکن ای کشیده از من دامن

کم بی تو نگشت جبر غمت پیراهن

از بهر خدا چه کرده ام با تو؟ بگو

بگذشت بلکه کس خوشش است الآ با من

SHAHAB KAGHAZI

A minor poet, probably active in the 13th century, probably from north-western Iran, about whom nothing is known. A handful of his poems have survived in the 14th-century anthology the *Nozhat al-Majales*.

You are avoiding me—be kind to me;
Without you I'm a mass of misery!
For God's sake tell me what I've done to you —
You're nice to everyone, except for me ...

کمال الدین اصفهانی

گل خوشست که چون رخش نکو باشد و نیست

چون دلبر من برنگ و بو باشد و نیست

صد روی فراهم آرد و هر سالی

باشد که یکی چو روی او باشد و نیست

با سردی وقت می تازه تر از من گل

از دست مدح جام می و من گل

زان پیش که ناگه شود از باد اجل

پیراهن عمر ما چو پیراهن گل

کس نیست که تا بر وطن خود گرید

بر حال تباه مردم بد گرید

دی بر سر مردی دو صد شیون بود

امروز یکی نیست که بر صد گرید

KAMALADDIN ESMAIL

The son of the poet Jamaladdin, Kamaladdin Esmail lived at the time of the Mongol devastation of Iran. When the Mongol garrison that had been left behind to hold Esfahan after its sack in 1237 was slaughtered in an uprising of the town's citizens, Kamaladdin wrote the third of the quatrains translated here. The Mongols retook the city later and he was tortured to death.

A rose-bush saw my dear belovèd's face
And wished its own face were as fresh and sweet;
Each year it brought a hundred faces forth —
Not one of them with her face could compete.

★

Live with your belovèd—sweeter than the flowers,
Live with joy and wine—at ease among the flowers;
Before we know, death's wind will tear the shirt
Of our short life—just as it tears the flowers'.

★

No man who's weeping for his country will complain
To see the overthrow of its oppressors' reign;
Two hundred wept for every man they killed, but now
Not one man weeps although a hundred men are slain.

سراجی سگزی

حال شب من که از سحر بیزار است
چشمم به ره است تا سحر بیدار است

گفتی که ز دوریم به خواهی مُرد‌ن
مُرد‌ن سهلست، زیستن دشوار است

SERAJI SEGZI

A 13th-century poet born near Nayshapour in Khorasan, active in
Makran (southern Iran and southern Pakistan) and northern India.

My watchful eyes know how I spend each night
That crawls reluctantly to dawn's first light.
At parting you said, 'Death is all I ask' —
Death would be easy; life is the harder task.

افضل الدین کاشانی

افضل چه نشسته‌ای که یاران رفتند
ماندی تو پیاده و سواران رفتند
در باغ نماند غیر زاغ و زغنی
سیمین بدنان سمن عذاران رفتند

پستیم چو خاک و سبز پلید نی ایمنت
پستیم ز عشق و هوس مند ایمنت
با این همه در دم نام درمان بریم
حقا که کمال در دم نه ایمنت

افضل دیدی که آنچه دیدی هیچ‌ست
سرتاسر آفاق دویدی هیچ‌ست
هر چیز که گفتی و شنیدی هیچ‌ست
وآن نیز که در کنج خزیدی هیچ‌ست

AFZALADDIN

A poet-philosopher from Kashan who was active during the first half of the 13th century. Some of the quatrains ascribed to him are also ascribed to other poets, including Omar Khayyam.

Why wait here, Afzal, now your friends have gone?
You're left behind on foot—they've ridden on.
Black crows and kites usurp the garden now
Where once their jasmine and their silver shone.

★

We are base, and this is true nobility;
We are drunk with love, and this is true sobriety;
With all we suffer here we seek no remedy —
This is the true perfection of adversity.

★

Afzal, you see that all you've seen is nothing,
That all the world through which you've been is nothing,
That all you've said and heard men say is nothing.
And creeping piously away is nothing.

★

آنانکه مقیم حضرت جانانند

یادش نکنند و بر زبان کم رانند

وآنان که به مثل ملهی بادانا اند

دورند از او از آن نیامیانش خوانند

آنها که درآمدند و درجوش شدند

نقشی از طرب به نوش شدند

خوردند پیاله‌ای و مدهوش شدند

در خاک ابد جمله هم آغوش شدند

هر نقش که بر تخته هستی پیدا ست

آن صورت آن کیست کاین نقش آرا ست

دریای کهن چو بر زند موجی نو

موجش خوانند و در حقیقت دریا ست

Those close to Him make little of the fact,
His is a name they almost never mention;
The windy ones who screech like fifes live far
From Him; that's why they're screeching—for attention.

★

All those who came here once so desperate
For wine, for pleasure, the belovèd's charms —
They drank one glass and sank down to the ground
Clasped pell-mell and forever in its arms.

★

Whatever images appear
Are images of Him who gave
Those images existence here:
The sea's depths rise, men say 'a wave' —
Each new wave in reality
Is nothing but the ancient sea.

رومی

گر با تو بوم نخنبم از یاری‌ها
ور بی تو بوم نخنبم از زاری‌ها
سبحان‌الله هر دو شب بدریم
تو فرق نگر میان بیداری‌ها

عشق آمد و شد چو خونم اندر رگ و پوست
تا کرد مرا خالی و پر کرد ز دوست
اجزای وجودم همگی دوست گرفت
نامی‌ست ز من بر من و باقی همه اوست

ما کار و دکان و پیشه را سوخته‌ایم
شعر و غزل و دو بیتی آموخته‌ایم
در عشق که او جان و دل و دیده ماست
جان و دل و دیده هر سه بر دوخته‌ایم

RUMI

One of the most celebrated of Persian poets, also known as Mowlavi. Born in Balkh in Afghanistan, he and his family moved westwards while he was still a boy, settling at Konya in Turkey. Here Rumi, like his father before him, acquired a reputation as an orthodox theologian until his life was transformed by a meeting with a wandering dervish, Shams-e Tabrizi. After this Rumi gave himself enthusiastically to sufism and his extremely voluminous writings are among the most admired sufi texts. He founded the order of the whirling dervishes and died in 1273. His great work is the six volume compendium of sufi doctrine and anecdotes, the *Masnavi-ye Ma'navi*. The quatrains translated here are from his collection of shorter poems, the Divan-e Shams-e Tabrizi. The second of them is also attributed to *Abu Sa'id Abul Khayr*.

The nights I spend with you, love will not let me sleep —
The nights I lie alone, I lie awake and weep;
With you or without you God knows I stay awake —
But look what different forms a sleepless night can take!

⋆

Like blood beneath my skin, within my veins, love came;
Now emptied of myself my friend fills all my frame;
My friend fills out my limbs, my life—he's all I am
And all that still remains of me in me's my name.

⋆

Profession, profit, trade are what we've burned;
Song, poetry, and verse are what we've learned;
We've given heart and soul and sight to love
And heart and soul and sight are what we've earned.

عارف

یک عالم از آب و گل بپرداخته‌اند
خود را به میان ما درانداخته‌اند
خود می‌گویند راز و خود می‌شنوند
زین آب و گلی بها به بر ساخته‌اند

بیمار توام، روی توام درمانست
جان داروی مشتاقان رخ جانانست
بشتاب که جانم به لب آمد بی تو
دریاب مرا، که بیش نتوان دانست

اول قدم از عشق تو را ندانستنست
جان بایست و با بلا سرشتنست
اول اینست و آخرش، چیستی دانی
خود را ز خودی خود بپرداختنست

ERAQI

c. 1213–69. Born in Hamadan, in western Iran, he travelled to India—
where he received instruction as a sufi—Turkey, Egypt and Syria: he
died in Damascus. He became famous in his own lifetime as a sufi
sheikh and mystical poet. By Eraqi's time the habit of writing mystical
verse with a quasi-erotic vocabulary, often homosexual at least by impli-
cation, had become widespread and much of his verse, particularly the
longer lyrical pieces, is of this kind. There are various stories about his
extravagant attachments to handsome young men, and though recent
scholarship tends to regard them with doubt, certainly some of his
poems make the stories' existence understandable.

He makes a world of water and of earth
In which He hides Himself; the mystery
He speaks, He hears. This water and this earth
Are the excuse for His soliloquy.

    ★

I'm sick—my only medicine is your face
(The right prescription in a lover's case);
But hurry now, my soul's already leaving —
Save me, or I'll have sunk without a trace.

    ★

In love the first step is to bow the head,
To risk your soul, acquaint yourself with dread:
This is the first—do you know what the last is?
To get yourself to treat your Self as dead.

مجذوبِ مِگر

میامد و در دیدهٔ ما می‌نگریست
می‌رفت و دگر سویِ قفا می‌نگریست

از عشوهٔ خویشتن خوشش می‌آمد
یا از رهِ مرحمت به ما می‌نگریست

ای خاک زِ دردِ دل نمی‌یارم گفت
کامروزِ اجل ز تو چه کوه به نهفت

دام دلِ عالمی فتاد و در دام
دلبندِ خلایقی در آغوشِ تو خفت

MAJD-E HAMGAR

A poet from Fars, the country's central province; his family claimed descent from the Sasanian rulers of pre-Islamic Iran. He lived mostly in Shiraz, and died in 1287.

As he went by he slyly glanced across at me
    And when he'd passed he looked back once again;
Now was he just enjoying his flirtatiousness
    Or did he feel real pity for my pain?

    ★

O Earth, my heart's grief thwarts whatever I might say —
How priceless is the jewel Death hides in you today!
The snare of all the world's hearts falls into your snare,
And in your arms sleeps one who stole all hearts away.

سعدی گیلانی

ما کی برای دل چنین خونخوار شوی
در دست ستمگری گرفتار شوی

آنگه دانی که دل چه پرده ست به تو
کز غفلت خواب عشق بیدار شوی

SA'D GILANI

A poet of whom virtually nothing is known, though his name implies he was from Gilan, a province bordering on the southern shores of the Caspian. Two of his *rubaiyat* are included in the *Nozhat al-Majales* (*c.* 1330), so this gives an approximate *terminus ante quem* for his dates.

How much more wretchedness
           for your wretched heart's sake?
How much imprisonment
           are you prepared to take?
You know your heart's record —
           rouse yourself, snap yourself
Out of love's sluttish sleep;
           you're better off awake.

صدر رنجبانی

با تو غم دل گفته، یا رب منم این؟

بوسیده عقیق نفته، یا رب منم این؟

دیدار تو ام، ز دو حاصل نشد ای

با تو به نشاط خفته، یا رب منم این؟

SADR-E ZANJANI

This poet has poems in the *Nozhat al-Majales*. It is possible that he is the same man as the vizir to the late 13th-century Mongol prince Gaykhatu, called Sadr-e Zanjani, who was best known for his unsuccessful attempt to introduce paper money into Iran; this caused such ferocious resistance that not even the Mongols were able to force the reform through. Zanjan—Zangan is another form of the same name—is in western Iran.

To talk to you about my heart's distress,
                    O God can this be me?
And then to kiss your agate lips no less,
                    O God can this be me?
For me to glimpse you, even from afar,
                    was once impossible —
To sleep with you, to know such happiness,
                    O God, can this be me?

علاء الدوله سمنانی

صدخانه گر بطاعت آباد کنی

زآن به نبود که خاطری شاد کنی

گر بنده کنی بلطف آزادی را

به زانکه هزار بنده آزاد کنی

ALA'AL-DOWLEH SEMNANI

A poet of the 13th–14th centuries from Semnan, a town to the east of
Tehran. He was born into a rich and powerful family but became a sufi
and donated his inherited wealth to sufi institutions and individuals.

Better gladden a single heart than build
A hundred houses out of 'charity';
Better enslave one free man with your kindness
Than free a thousand men from slavery.

خسرو دهلوی

ای از تو مرا امید بهبودی نه
با من تو چنانکه پیش از این بودی نه

می‌دانم که عهد و پیمان مرا
در هم شکنی، ولی به این زودی نه

یاد آیدت آن مهر و وفاداری‌ها
وان درحق من ملطف غمخواری‌ها

اکنون بتصور چنان یاری‌ها
پاییم و شب دراز و بیداری‌ها

KHOSROW DEHLAVI

Khosrow Dehlavi's parents fled from Balkh to India at the time of the
Mongol invasion of Khorasan, and the poet was born in Delhi in 1253.
He spent most of his life in this city, and is considered one of the greatest
of Indian poets who wrote in Persian. He had a prolific output in almost
all genres of verse as well as in prose. He assiduously imitated the
acknowledged masters of poetry; he does however have a distinctive style,
characterized by an elegant and gentle sweetness, which in its turn influ-
enced later Persian-speaking poets of the sub-continent. He died in 1324.

There never was much hope for me with you —
The way you used to be could hardly last;
I knew you'd break the promises you gave,
But not that you would break them quite so fast.

★

Do you remember all that love and faithfulness?
Vows to be always there to share a friend's distress?
These days the image of fidelity like that
Is found in me, and endless nights, and wakefulness.

★

من بودم و دوش آن بت بنده‌نواز

از من همه لابه بود و از وی همه ناز

شب رفت و حدیث ما به پایان نرسید

شب را چه گنه؟ قصهٔ ما بود دراز

هوشم نه موافقان و خویشان بردند

این کج‌کلهان مو پریشان بردند

گویند چه‌ها تو دل بایشان دادی

بالله که من ندادم، ایشان بردند

ای باد که از کوی وفا می‌آیی

آلوده به بوی آشنا می‌آیی

زانگونه که نغز و جانفزا می‌آیی

من می‌دانم که از کجا می‌آیی

She spent last night with me
                    to tease her abject prey;
The more that I implored
                    the more she urged delay;
Our talk was still not done
                    when night had turned to day —
But do not blame the night
                    for we had much to say!

      ★

It's not my friends who snatched away my sense,
It was those rakish caps and tumbling curls that took it.
They say, 'Why did you give your heart to them?'
I didn't give it though, it was the girls that took it!

      ★

O Breeze, blown from the Street of Faithfulness
And mingled with the scent of one I know,
You come with such caressing gentleness
That all too well I realize whence you blow …

خواجوی کرمانی

بر گرد و شش چرخ چون نیابد دست

دل در بد و نیک دهر چون باید بست

این محنت و غم که هست پندار که نیست

وین عیش و طرب که نیست انگار که هست

KHAJU

Born in 1290 in Kerman in south-eastern Iran, he lived in various parts of the country until his death in 1352. In the latter part of his life he lived in Shiraz and is said to have been a friend of Hafez, the greatest of Iran's lyric poets.

    Since no hand halts the turning of Fate's wheel
And hearts must suit themselves to what the skies reveal —
    Think that the grief there is does not exist,
Imagine that your non-existent joys are real.

رکن صباین

گرت بجاه بود خوابگاه بسیط بهشت
وقت نگر بود فرش خاک و بالین خشت

از آن مال که آنرا نا پاک گذشت
بدان مال که آنرا نه پاک بهشت

مسافران بقا را چو نیست روی مقام
دو روزه منزل و آرامگاه چه خوب و چه زشت

ROKN-E SAYEN

A 14th-century poet from Khorasan, who worked at various courts including that of Shah Shoja', the patron of Hafez. He died around 1363.

If worldly wealth means that you sleep in luxury
Or if your pillow is the earth and poverty,
Don't gripe about the one for it will soon be past —
And don't congratulate yourself on what won't last:
Since pilgrim-souls have no abiding city here
What's there to boast of for two days? What's there to fear?

ابن یمین

سود دنیا و دین اگر خواهی
مایه هر دو شان نکوکاریست

راحت بندگان حق خواستن
عین تقوی و زهد و دینداریست

گر در خلد را کلیدی هست
بی نبخشیدن و کرم آزریست

مرا نام اگر نیک و گر بد بود
چو رفتم از آن چه فخر و چه عار

کسی را بود فخر و عار او بود
که ماند زمین در جهان یادگار

پس از من اگر بهتری باشد روا
چو من دامن افشانم این غبار

EBN-E YAMIN

1286–1367. He worked as a court poet in various parts of Iran, but was born and died in Khorasan. The frequent other-worldliness of his sentiments is a good object-lesson in showing how cautious it's necessary to be in interpreting this kind of poetry autobiographically—since superficially it would seem that a court life would be the last thing the author of such poems would want. Contempt for the court and fashion was itself a courtly, fashionable style.

To profit from this world and from religion
Know that the heart of both is man's benevolence,
To seek the rights and comfort of the poor
Will equal any self-denying ordinance —
And if there is a key to Heaven's gate
It's kindness, and a lack of all malevolence.

★

If I've a good name or an evil name
When I have left this world, what's that to me?
Theirs will be all the glory and the shame
If I've descendants living after me:
Whatever's said of me is all the same
When once I've shaken off this dust from me.

★

کسی که با تو نکویی کند چو بتوانی
در استمالت او کوش و درد در علاتش

وگر بدی کند اورا بزرگوار سپار
که روزگارت به سر درد بهر تو مکافاتش

دو قرص نان اگر گنده‌ام است اگرا جو
دو تای جامه اگر کهنه است اگر ازنو

به چار گوشه ایوان خود تخاطر جمع
که کس نگوید از اینجای خیز و آنجا رو

هزار بار نکوتر به نزد ابن یمین
رفوی مملکت که یقبا د و کنجره‌و

If anyone does good to you
Reward him all you're able to —
Leave one who hurts you to the world,
The world will see he gets his due.

★

Two loaves of bread—coarse barley or fine wheat—will do;
Likewise two sets of clothes suffice, worn out or new;
Contentment, and a corner I can call my own
Where no one says, 'You can't stay here, be off with you!'
Yamin prefers this—O a thousand times!—to glory;
To King Qobad's reign, and to splendid Khosrow's too.

حافظ

چون جا مه زرین بکشد آن مشکین خال

ماهی که نظیر خود ندارد به جمال

در سینه دلش ز نازکی بتوان دید

مانند به سنگ خاره در آب زلال

عمری پی مراد ضایع دارم

و ز دور فلک چیست کمی نافع دارم

با هر که بگفتم که ترا دوست شدم

شد دشمن من و ک چه طالع دارم

من حاصل عمر خود ندارم جز غم

در عشق ز نیک و بد ندارم جز غم

یک همدم با وفا ندیدم جز درد

یک مونس نامزد ندارم جز غم

HAFEZ

The most famous of Persian lyric poets, he lived from c. 1320–89, mostly in his birthplace, Shiraz. His great fame rests on his *ghazals*, which are so allusive and dense in their language, using the often arcane conventions of Persian lyric poetry with consummate dexterity, as to be virtually untranslatable. In a generally simpler style he also wrote a relatively small number of *rubaiyat*, versions of six of which are offered here.

A black mole graced his face; he stripped, and shone
Incomparable in splendor as the moon;
He was so slim his heart was visible,
As if clear water sluiced a granite stone.

★

Desire's destroyed my life; what gifts have I
Been given by the blindly turning sky?
And, such is my luck, everyone I said
'Dear friend' to loathed me by and by.

★

What does life give me in the end but sorrow?
What do love's good and evil send but sorrow?
I've only seen one true companion—pain,
And I have known no faithful friend but sorrow.

★

هر دوست که دم زد ز وفا دشمن شد

هر پاک روی که بود تر دامن شد

گویند شب آبستن دینت عجب

کو مرد ندید از چه آبستن شد

با می بکنار جوی می باید بود

وز غصه کناره جوی می باید بود

این مدت عمر ما چو گل ده روز است

خندان لب و تازه روی می باید بود

ای دوست دل از جفا دشمن درکش

با روی نکو شراب روشن درکش

با اهل هنر گوی گریبان بگشای

وز نااهلان تمام دامن درکش

Each 'friend' turned out to be an enemy,
Corruption rotted all their 'purity';
They say the night is pregnant with new times,
But since no men are here, how can that be?

*

With wine beside a gently flowing brook—this is best;
Withdrawn from sorrow in some quiet nook—this is best;
Our life is like a flower's that blooms for ten short days,
Bright laughing lips, a friendly, fresh-faced look—this is best.

*

My friend, hold back your heart from enemies,
Drink shining wine with handsome friends like these;
With art's initiates let down your hair —
Stay buttoned up with ignoramuses.

جهان خاتنم

گفتم که دگر چشم به بد نگه نکنم
صوفی شوم و گوش به منکر نکنم
دیدم که خلاف طبع موزون منست
توبت که دم که توبه دیگر نکنم

شبهای دراز بیشتر بیدارم
نزدیک سحر روی ببالین آرم
میپندارم که دیده بی دیدن دوست
در خواب رود خیال میپندارم

JAHAN KHATUN

An aristocrat of the 14th century, daughter of Jallaladdin Mas'ud Shah Inju, ruler of Fars, the central province of Iran; she lived chiefly in Shiraz, the provincial capital. Her *Divan* (collected poems), with an introduction by herself, has survived—a rare event for a Persian woman poet from before the 19th century. Various legends about her exist, including one that she had a lover at court with whom she exchanged poems and who died young. These poems to a 'lover' seem in fact to have been addressed to her step-mother whose early death was deeply mourned by the poet. An extremely scabrous poem by her contemporary, Obayd-e Zakani, implies that she was a prostitute, but as Obayd said this kind of thing about virtually everyone he mentioned, no credence need be given to it. She considerably outlived her family's fall from power (her father was murdered in a local *coup d'état*) and some of her poems complain of the difficulties of her later life.

I swore I'd never look at him again,
I'd be a sufi, deaf to sin's temptations;
I saw my nature wouldn't stand for it —
From now on I renounce renunciations.

★

For most of these long nights I stay awake
And go to bed as dawn begins to break;
I think that eyes that haven't seen their friend
Might get some sleep then … this is a mistake.

امیرشاهی

ما را چه از آن که هر کسی ما بیند

یک عیب که در ما بود او صد بیند

ما آینه ایم، هر که در ما نگرد

هم نیک و بدی که هست از خود بیند

AMIR SHAHI

A 15th-century poet who lived almost all his life in Sabzevar, a small town in Khorasan to the south of the Jaghatai mountains.

What's it to me if everyone looks down on me
And where I've one fault hundreds are suspected?
I'm just a mirror, and all those who frown on me
Are only seeing what's in them—reflected.

فغانی

ساقی قدحی که از میان خواهم رفت
آشفته و مست از جهان خواهم رفت

در آمدنم نبود از هیچ خبر
آن دم که روم نیز چنان خواهم رفت

FAGHANI

A 15th-century poet born in Shiraz who spent much of his life travelling
and looking for patrons in Khorasan and Azerbaijan. He lived into the
16th century and saw the establishment of the Safavid dynasty by Shah
Esmail (1501).

Bring wine, my boy—I'm dying now I know,
Blind-drunk is how I'll quit this earthly show;
I entered life completely ignorant
And that's precisely how I plan to go.

فیض ترتی

عشق من و حسن تو بهم ساخته اند

پیوسته یکدگر نظر باخته اند

فارغ ز من و تو در فسانخه دِل

بنشسته و طرح صحبت انداخته اند

FAYZI (OF TORBAT)

A 15th-century poet from Torbat in eastern Iran. He is not to be confused with the much more illustrious Indian poet of the same name.

Your Beauty and my Love for you agree,
Sat side by side where nothing comes between them —
Together now, and far from you and me,
They sit and talk where we have never seen them.

وحشی بافقی

گر با تو گهی نظر کنم سّم پنهانی
لازم نبود طبع خود رنجانی
من بودم و دیده‌ی چو این هم منّت است
آن نیز تو یاران دگر ارزانی

ای صبا خواجه را زبند و بگو
که در مدح می‌توانم گفت
ور به رنجشی و ناخوشی افتد
هیچ هم غم نمی‌توانم گفت

VAHSHI

A 16th-century poet from the small town of Bafgh, which lies between Yazd and Kerman in south-eastern Iran. His poetry was mostly written in the service of various members of the ruling Safavid family, including Shah Tahmasp (1524–76; known to English travellers of the period as 'Shah Thomas'). Vahshi's name means "the wild one," but his poetry could hardly be more decorous. He died in 1583.

If secretly I've glanced at you
Don't be annoyed with me: it's true
That kind of glance is not allowed —
But all the others do it too!

★

Sweet breeze, inform my noble lord from me
That panegyrics are what I excel at,
And if he gets obstreperous and rude
Say satire's also something I do well at.

فیض

آن روز که کرد دشمن من و تو

بردند ز دست اختیار من و تو

فارغ بنشین که کارساز جهان

پیش از من و تو ساخته کار من و تو

FAYZI (OF AGRA)

Born in Agra in 1556, he became one of the most admired of the Persian-speaking poets of India. He was appointed Poet Laureate to the Moghul emperor Akbar; his brother was Akbar's chief minister and wrote a biography of the emperor, the *Akbarnameh*. Fayzi died in 1595.

From that day He roughed out the scene of me and you,
What our hands do can't intervene in me and you;
Rest easy now—since God had seen to me and you
Long, long before there'd ever been a me and you.

سحابی

عشق آمد و هر سر زبان و هر بن بسوخت
جزو جهان به هر چه که بنمود بسوخت
یعنی بجهان هستیم آتش زد
هر چیزی در و سوختنی بود بسوخت

ما اصل بت از بت شکنان یافته‌ایم
اسرار دل از طعنه زنان یافته‌ایم
آن راز نهان که دوست می فرمود
در پرده طعن دشمنان یافته‌ایم

SAHABI

He was born in Shushtar in the southwest of Iran. He spent over forty years of his life in the Shi'i holy city of Najaf, in Iraq, where he died in 1601.

Love came—and burned out all I'd lost and all I'd earned
Till nothing but Eternity could be discerned;
I mean that all my World of Being was burned up,
Whatever in that world was burnable was burned.

★

Iconoclasts have taught me what an idol is,
I learnt love's lore from those who scorned and haunted me;
That secret the Eternal Friend imparts to us
I learnt within the tents of those who taunted me.

یک خانه‌ات اَپُر ز کتاب تُهی است
سُودت نکند چو کیسهٔ سیم تُهی است
زر باید، زر که ضرب شاهی دارد
معشوقه چه داند که «فان قیل بویُوست»

در نغمهٔ دهر که نسازت ترا
از بیشرمی بلند آواز ترا
در مرتبهٔ تر از و از نفت هنر
هر سر که تُهی از آن سرافراز ترا

ANONYMOUS (BEFORE 1330)

Your house is crammed with theology books—so what?
They're useless without money—which you haven't got.
Gold's what you need, coins of the realm! Does your girl care
About your *De Potentia* and all such rot?

★

The world's a scale where men are weighed —
The worse they are the more they boast;
But that's the way that scales are made —
The emptier pan's the uppermost.

Index

A Note on the Type

The type in this book was set in a digitized version of Plantin, a typeface designed by F. H. Pierpont. Pierpont was an American who worked for the Monotype Corporation in England from 1899-1936. He was a manager at their works in Surrey and mostly adapted existing type designs to suit Monotype machines. However, in 1913, he oversaw the design of the Plantin typeface, which was among the first to be specifically designed for mechanical composition.

Plantin was named after Christopher Plantin, a Frenchman who was one of the foremost printer/publishers in 16th century northern Europe.

The Persian text was calligraphed by Amir Hossein Tabnak. He was born in Tehran in 1935 and was a founding member of the Iranian Society of Calligraphers. He has had numerous publications and exhibitions in Iran, Japan and the US and currently teaches at the Smithsonian Institution in Washington, D.C.

About the Translator

Dick Davis was born in Portsmouth, England, in 1945 and educated at King's College, Cambridge (B.A. and M.A. in English Literature) and at the University of Manchester (PhD. in Medieval Persian Literature). He has taught at the universities of Tehran, Durham, Newcastle and California-Santa Barbara, and is currently associate Professor of Persian at Ohio State University. He lived for eight years in Iran (1970–78), as well as for periods in Greece and Italy. He is a Fellow of the Royal Society of Literature.

TRANSLATIONS FROM PERSIAN
The Conference of the Birds by Farid'uddin Attar
(1984, with Afkham Darbandi)
The Legend of Seyavash by Ferdowsi (1992)
My Uncle Napoleon by Iraj Pezeshkzad (1996)
Borrowed Ware: Medieval Persian Epigrams (1996)
The Lion and the Throne:
Stories from the Shahnameh of Ferdowsi, Volume I (1997)

TRANSLATIONS FROM ITALIAN
The Little Virtues by Natalia Ginzburg (1985)
The City and The House by Natalia Ginzburg (1986)

POETRY
In the Distance (1975)
Seeing the World (1980)
The Covenant (1984)
Devices and Desires: New and Selected Poems (1989)
A Kind of Love: Selected and New Poems (1991)
Touchwood: Poems 1991-1994 (1996)

EDITIONS
Selected Writings of Thomas Traherne (1980)
The Rubaiyat of Omar Khayyam
translated by Edward FitzGerald (1989)

CRITICISM
Wisdom and Wilderness: The Achievement of Yvor Winters (1983)
Epic and Sedition: The Case of Ferdowsi's Shahnameh (1992)

Other Books From Mage Publishers

The Lion and the Throne:
Stories from the Shahnameh of Ferdowsi, Volume I
prose rendition by Ehsan Yarshater / translation by Dick Davis

The Persian Garden: Echoes of Paradise
Mehdi Khansari / M. R. Moghtader / Minouch Yavari

My Uncle Napoleon
Iraj Pezeshkzad / translated by Dick Davis

Tales of Two Cities: A Persian Memoir
Abbas Milani

New Food of Life: Ancient Persian and
Modern Iranian Cooking and Cermenonies
Najmieh Batmanglij

Persian Cooking For A Healthy Kitchen
Najmieh Batmanglij

The Persian Bazaar: Veiled Space of Desire
Mehdi Khansari / Minouch Yavari

Lost Treasures of Persia: Persian Art in the Hermitage Museum
Vladamir Loukonine / Anatoli Ivanov

The Art of Persian Music
Jean During / Zia Mirabdolbaghi / Dariush Safvat

Stories from Iran: A Chicago Anthology 1921-1991
edited by Heshmat Moayyad

Savushun: A Novel about Modern Iran
Simin Daneshvar / translated by M.R. Ghanoonparvar

Sutra and Other Stories
Simin Daneshvar / translated by Amin Neshati & Hasan Javadi

King of the Benighted
Manuchehr Irani / translated by Abbas Milani